KETO DIET
COOKBOOK FOR WOMEN OVER 50

*The Complete Beginner's Guide To The Ketogenic Diet For Seniors
With 200 Easy And Delicious Recipes To Lose Weight Quickly
And Finally Regain Confidence.
(30-Day Meal Plan Included)*

MARIA J. VICKERS

Table Of Contents

CHAPTER 14: SNACKS AND DESSERT RECIPES............. 122

CONCLUSION 137

Introduction

All of us gradually get older. It is a sure fact of our life. But even though we are aging all the time, we do not need to be old, not yet anyway. Because believe me, it is possible to be active, vibrant at fifty and beyond if you make some smart choices and take care of yourself. And deciding to follow the keto way of life is the smartest choice of everyone that could ever make when choosing the right and suitable diet at this age. The keto diet isn't just good for weight loss, although that is probably its most important and noticeable feature. It gives so much more to our body while helping us lose and then maintain our weight.

As I write this book, my main objective is to help women who reached their senior years but still want to live young, healthy, and more active. If you're one of them and want to try this Ketogenic Diet that was made mostly for age above 50, you are on the right page!

When the keto diet helps you lose weight, it also reduces your risk of cardiovascular disease. When you lose weight and decrease the amount of fat and cholesterol in the body, there will be less accumulation in the arteries, and the blood will naturally flow better with less restriction.

Being overweight can cause high blood pressure. Losing weight plus being at a healthy weight will ease the strain on your heart. If the blood pressure is not pumping too high, it will not cause weak arteries' weak spots. If there are no soft spots, then there is no place for plaque to collect.

For you, who are above 50 but want to be better and healthier, adopting the keto way of life will help eliminate your kidneys' problems and improve their function. Kidney stones and gout are caused mainly by the elevation of certain urine chemicals that help create uric acid, which we eliminate in the bathroom. When ketones begin to rise, the acid in urine will briefly increase as your body begins to eliminate all waste products from the metabolized fats. However, the level will decrease and remain lower than before as long as you are on the keto diet.

The best overall advantage of the keto lifestyle is that it will lower your overall weight, positively affecting your entire body. Losing weight will mean freedom from the effects of obesity, which can help eliminate metabolic syndrome and Type 2 Diabetes. The condition known as metabolic syndrome happens when the body becomes resistant to insulin, and the insulin your body produces is not recognized by the cells in your body. That causes the body to store your excess blood sugar as fat in your body, especially around the stomach area. When we begin the keto diet and enter Ketosis, the body will be forced to use these fat stores for energy, and the body's production of insulin will be returned to normal. The number of proteins in the diet will help our muscles keep their strength and tone and not begin to wither as so often happens in older women.

The keto diet will result in increased brain function and the ability to focus. The brain typically uses sugar to fuel its processes, but the consumption of sugar has its problems. The mind can easily switch to using ketones for fuel and energy. Always remember that ketones are the by-product of Ketosis that makes you burn fat.

Inflammation is a part of life, especially for people over the age of fifty. There is the right kind of inflammation, such as when white blood cells rush to a particular body area to kill an infection. Most older people are plagued by the wrong forms of inflammation, which make your joints swell and cause early morning stiffness. Losing weight will help to eliminate inflammation in the body.

This ultimate guide can give you full knowledge regarding Keto Diet and answer the questions that are keeping you from sailing to your new healthy Keto lifestyle. Trust me; you don't want to miss this opportunity! Full-packed with Keto knowledge and, of course, the highlights to this are giving you simple, fast, and easy-to-follow Keto recipes, and a 30-day meal plan for men and women exclusively made separately, that will complete your Keto-journey!

Following the keto diet will mean that you will eat less food, but it will be more filling and more nutritious. When you eat fats and proteins instead of carbs, you will feel fuller much longer with less food. Lowering your caloric will keep your weight loss, and less weight will make you healthier. It will also slash your risk of developing certain diseases and will minimize the effects of others. These are the life improvements that the keto lifestyle has to offer you.

CHAPTER 1:

Important Tips for The Ketogenic Diet After 50 Years Old

The Keto diet gets popular as it's a very effective way of weight loss, but research also shows that it doesn't only help you lose weight but also benefits your health greatly. When you use fat as fuel, your body becomes much active and sustainable. The extra energy will help you do workouts and improve your stamina.

Benefits of Keto Diet for Women Over 50

Energy level rise

Women after 50 don't have the same level of energy as 30 years women have. They struggle with doing the workout, but Keto has gotten your back. It helps in raising your energy level, so you don't feel bad about being weak. In the first days, you may feel so exhausted, tired but with time your energy level rises and gives you strength, and your mind also works best with proper focus on the tasks you do.

Anxiety and depression diminish

The Keto diet also helps in reducing anxiety. This is due to the high intake of fat and a low level of sugar. A recent study also showed that the women who were on a Keto diet were not facing anxiety and depression, but those who were not having this diet were more prone to depression.

Protection against Type 2 diabetes

The Keto diet also cuts your sugar intake to less than 20g, and it helps in maintaining your blood sugar level if you are a diabetes patient. Type 2 patients also manage to control their blood sugar when put into the Keto diet. This is very beneficial for women who have diabetes, and they are struggling with their weight as well.

Healthy body and lifestyle

Your life gets healthier when you are on a keto diet. Your intake of fat becomes more, and you consume very less sugar and carbs. The keto diet also helps to reduce Fatty liver disease and other inflammation, which occurs due to eating more sweeteners and an unhealthy diet. Your body becomes fit, and you start living a healthy lifestyle.

Sound sleep time

Women who are on a Keto diet tell that they feel much satisfied and sound while sleeping, and their sleep cycle also improves drastically. Although in the first days you feel restlessness and tiredness with insomnia after 4-5 days, your sleep cycle gets better, and you would sleep longer, relaxed, and fulfilled when you wake up.

Keto diet may help in the treatment of cancer

A Keto diet is also a way to treat very serious diseases, and cancer is one of them. It stops the growth of the tumor. The research showed that the ketones bodies may provide energy to your body without being the food for the cancerous tumor.

Cravings diminish

The benefit of a Keto diet is that you become habitual of the lifestyle you follow during this diet. You start controlling your blood sugar level, which helps in controlling cravings. You also feel that you can go long without having sweets or Sugar. Intermitted fasting becomes common among women who have been on a Keto diet, which is very useful for your body.

Keto can improve your heart health and sharpen your brain

It may look strange that a diet filled with fats is beneficial for the heart, but it is true. In one year's study, 22 out of 26 cases of cardiovascular showed an improvement in their health conditions. Notably, these women experienced a Keto diet and intermittent fasting. Your brain also sharpens when you are on a Keto diet; there is a lot of evidence which are showing how significant this diet is. The brain works more efficiently on ketones than blood sugar.

Improve chances of conceiving

A Keto diet is one of the best ways to improve the chances of conceiving for women. Most women are worried about issues steaming from PCOS, which can cause a stop to your evolution cycle and make pregnancy impossible. But, recent studies showed that the women who were facing issues conceiving started conceiving when they chose a keto diet for themselves.

Keto can also help in different diseases, and most importantly, it helps improve your acne, which is normally a big hassle for women. It is also a cure for polycystic ovary syndrome and nervous system disorders.

Improve Neurological health

Aging can put several neurological health risks, which include dementia and Alzheimer's disease. Research shows that it happens due to the increase of sugar levels in the bloodstream, which causes these neurological diseases. Keeping these levels normal can help your brain work faster and improves your memory. Keto makes your neurological health better by reducing the intake of sugar in your diet. Weight gain is common for women when they are 50 or beyond, and this causes stress and neurological problem to some women. A Keto diet is the best way to improve your mental health and live life as you have dreamt of.

Combats Fatigue

Getting older and having a slower metabolism is a feeling which makes yourself so tired often, and you want to look younger and active at the same time. The best way to combat Fatigue is to exercise and keep excess weight off. When you are on a Keto-friendly diet, you can snack as much as you can but definitely with the right foods. Your target can be burning your stubborn belly fats first because belly fats lead to visceral fats which squeezes internal organ and protect them from functioning in the right way.

Lowers your blood pressure

Hypertension and increased blood pressure lead to significant risk factors for many diseases like kidney failure, stroke, and heart disease. A Keto diet helps you lower your blood pressure and prevent you from these diseases. What do you need when you have a diet that is giving you a chance to live a longer life?

From a ketogenic diet, you get a chance to lose weight in days with a proper diet plan, which will allow your body to work in a better condition.

When you cut carbs, it becomes easier for you to lose weight in days. Every woman wants to look pretty and beautiful, and you also want to have a diet plan which is quick and easy for you to follow. Even though a low-carb diet helps you lose weight in a short period but it has long-lasting benefits.

Improve the functioning of the immune system

The Keto diet is very advantageous for women because it provides women with a lot of health benefits. The concept of intermitted fasting in this diet is a blessing for women because it protects their immune system and reduces the risk of breast cancer. The other risks of women-related diseases are also minimized when they are on a Keto diet.

Heal bone diseases like Arthritis

Studies revealed that women over 50 who have arthritis were following a keto diet. Guess what? They healed from this diet, and their pain was gone away when they followed a specific diet plan and cut off carbs from their diet. Isn't it magical? Yes, you can also heal by following a keto diet. Some of you might be wondering if it would work on you, there is a great possibility that it will work on you.

Researchers have proved by several pieces of evidence that the keto diet is a perfect diet for women, and it is safe to start even if you are over 50. There is no harm to this diet if you are doing it right. You have to just make your mind and beat the aging stress from your mind. You would feel younger and healthier when you are on a Keto diet. It is a complete package which not only protects you from diseases but also gives you a chance to regain your energy and maintain your ideal body weight.

CHAPTER 2:

Basics of Ketogenic Diet

A ketogenic diet is classified as a deficient carbohydrate diet. The diet is high in fat, moderate in protein, and low in carbs. It makes your body a fat-burning unit. There's a far more theoretical explanation, but you essentially force the body to generate ketones for energy in the liver. On the contrary, consuming high-carbs foods and sugars in your body will make glucose and increase insulin levels.

The ratio is predicted to be about 80% fat and 20% protein. This is the first two days' guideline. When in ketogenic conditions, you have to increase the consumption of protein and reduce the Fat; the ratio is roughly 65 percent Fat, 30 % Protein, and 5 percent carbs. protein is strengthened to regenerate the tissue of the muscle. When you take carbohydrates in your body, it triggers an insulin spike, which means insulin (helps store amino acids, glycogen, and excess calories as fat) is released by your pancreas, so common sense is that if you remove carbs, you won't store excess calories like fat.

Your body now has no carbs as a source of energy, so your body needs to find a new source. This works perfectly if you want to lose fat. The body breaks down the body's fat and uses it instead of carbs as energy. This condition is referred to as ketosis. This is the condition in which you want your body to be, and it makes sense if you want to lose fat while holding your muscle.

Now about the diet and how to prepare it. A gram of protein per pound of lean mass must be taken AT Least. This helps to recover and rebuild muscle tissue after exercise and so on. Recall the ratio? fat 65 percent and protein 30 percent. If you weigh 150 pounds, that is 150 g of protein a day. X4 (calorie per gram of protein) is 600 calories. The remaining calories should be fat. If your caloric preservation is 3,000, you need to eat about 500 fewer, which means that about 1900 calories have to come from fats if you have 2500 calories a day! You have to consume fats to maintain your body and remove fat! You have to eat fats that are the maxim of this diet! The value of eating food fats and keto diets is that you're not going to feel hungry. fat digestion is sluggish, which works for your benefit and allows you to feel complete.

This is Monday-Friday, then "carbohydrate" on the weekend. After your last training on Friday, the carbs begin. You must take a liquid carbohydrate, and your whey shakes post-training. This helps produce an insulin spike, which allows your body to urgently repair, which develops muscles and fills up its glycogen stores. Eat what you want during this stage: pasta, pizzas, ice cream, crisps. This will help you, as it will feed your body for the next week and restore your body's nutritional needs. On Sunday, the no high carb fat moderate protein diet begins. The ideal cure is to hold your body in ketosis and burn fat as energy.

The figures for women are also higher. Women have other female-related influences for which we must deal with because of our child-bearing bodies. Higher estrogen levels and various female hormones already have a higher fat proportion of our body. Obesity is described medically as having an index of over 30 percent (BMI). We are now more than 50 years of age. We started searching for a better way to get closer to food.

Although Ketogenic is new to many, it was established in the 1920s. Studies concluded that weight loss was reported, and participants could eat less food. Keto lifestyle may have a beneficial impact on serious health problems such as cardiovascular and diabetes have been confirmed. It increases HDL Cholesterol levels.

How Does the Ketogenic Diet Works?

The time has come for you to get the answer to the question that has been lingering in your mind from the time you heard about the keto diet; 'how does a keto diet work?'

Here is how.

The power behind the Ketogenic diet's ability to help you lose weight and have better health comes from one simple action that the diet initiates in your body once you start following it. This simple action is how the keto diet changes your metabolism from burning carbohydrates for energy to burning fats for energy.

What does that have to do with weight loss and better health?

Let me break it down for you.

- Burning carbohydrates for energy

Most of the food we eat follows the food pyramid recommended by the USDA some few decades ago. The pyramid puts carbohydrates at the bottom of the pyramid and fats at the top of the pyramid, which essentially means that carbohydrates form the bulk of the foods we eat.

What many of us don't know is that when you consume a diet that is high in carbohydrates, two things normally happen.

- One, your body takes the just consumed carbohydrates and converts them into glucose which is the easiest molecule that your body can convert to use as energy (glucose is your body's primary source of energy, as it gets chosen over any other energy source in your body).

- Secondly, your body produces insulin for the sole purpose of it moving the glucose from your bloodstream into your cells where it can be used as energy.

There is more that goes unnoticed though:

Since your body gets its energy from glucose (which is mostly in huge amounts owing to the fact that we eat lots of high-carb food 3-6 times a day), it doesn't need any other source of energy. In fact, many are the times when glucose is in excess, something that prompts the body to convert Dietary glucose into glycogen to be stored in the liver and muscle cells. What this simple explanation means is that with a high-carb diet, your body is essentially in what we refer to as a Fat-storing mode. It stores this excess fat so that it can use it when starved from its primary source of energy; glucose. Unfortunately, since we don't give ourselves enough breaks from food, we end up being in this constant fat-storing mode that ultimately causes weight gain.

- Burning fats for energy

As you now know, the Ketogenic diet is a low carb, high fat, and moderate protein diet. So, when you start following a Ketogenic diet, what typically happens is, your intake of carbohydrates is kept at a low. In other words, it inverts the USDA food pyramid, something that literally 'inverts/reverses' the effects of a high-carb diet.

How exactly does it do that?

Well, when you limit your carb intake greatly, you starve the body of its primary source of energy, something that initiates the process that the body has always been preparing for through its energy storage processes. More specifically, the body starts by metabolizing glycogen with the help of glucagon hormone (the process takes place in the liver). And with support from the human growth hormone, cortisol, and catecholamines (norepinephrine to be more specific), the body starts releasing Fatty acids for use as energy in different body parts. But since Fatty acids cannot be used by every cell in the body, the body is also forced to transport some of the Fatty acids to the liver where they are broken down in a series of metabolic processes known as ketosis to produce 3 ketone bodies. Therefore, Ketosis is a natural process that your body activates when your energy intake is low for the purpose of helping you to survive. The three ketones that are formed when Fatty acids are converted are:

- Acetone.
- Beta-hydroxybutyric acid (BHB)
- Acetoacetate (AcAc)

Many of your body cells (including the brain cells) can use BHB for energy, as it is water-soluble, something that makes it very much like glucose in that it can cross the blood-brain barrier. The more ketones the body cells use for energy, the more fat you are burning, and ultimately, the more weight you stand to gain. Keep in mind that you are also taking lots of Dietary fats. The reason for taking lots of Dietary fats is to fill you up fast, make you stay full for longer, and accustom the body cells to using fatty acids and ketones for energy so that when the deficit created by Dietary fats kicks in (because you are unlikely to eat so much fats to the point of meeting your body's energy requirements- unless you are gluttonous), you begin burning stored body fat immediately, as opposed to starting with glycogen. Moderate intake of protein also helps you to get filled fast and to stay full for longer. Keeping your protein intake moderate is therefore vital, as any excess may end up causing you to get out of ketosis, as excess protein may be metabolized to glucose in a process known as gluconeogenesis. This essentially means a Ketogenic diet makes your body a fat-burning machine, as it relies primarily on fats (both Dietary and stored body fat—though you want to get your body to burn as much of the stored boy fat as possible).

Ketosis helps you get rid of excessive fats in your body, which not only reduces your weight in an immense way but also betters your health by protecting you from various diseases as you will see.

To attain ketosis, you know that your intake of fats should be high, intake of carbs low, and intake of proteins moderate. But what exactly does high, low, and moderate translate to in calorie terms? In simpler terms, in what ratios should you take carbs, fats, and proteins? This gives rise to several types/approaches/schools of thought regarding the ratios:

Who Invented This Diet?

The ketogenic diet traces its roots to the treatment of epilepsy. Surprisingly this goes all the way back to 500 BC, when ancient Greeks observed that fasting or eating a ketogenic diet helped reduce epileptic seizures. In modern times, the ketogenic diet was reintroduced in the practice of medicine to treat children with epilepsy.

What is Ketosis?

Ketosis is a metabolic state where the body is efficiently using fat for energy. In a regular diet, carbohydrates produce glucose, which is used to provide energy. Glucose is stored in the body in fat cells that travel via the bloodstream. People gain weight when there is fatter stored than being used as energy.

Glucose is formed through the consumption of sugar and starch. Namely carbohydrates. The sugars may be in the form of natural Sugars from fruit or milk, or they may be formed from processed Sugar. Starches like pasta, rice, or starchy vegetables like potatoes and corn, form glucose as well. The body breaks down the sugars from these foods into glucose. Glucose and insulin combined to help to carry glucose into the bloodstream so the body can use glucose as energy. The glucose that is not used is stored in the liver and muscles.

In order for the body to supply ketones for use as fuel, the body must use up all the reserves of glucose. In order to do this, there must be a condition of the body of starvation low carbohydrates, passing, or strenuous exercise. A very low carb diet, the production of ketones what her to feel the body and brain.

Ketones are produced from the liver when there is not enough glucose in the body to provide energy. When insulin levels are low, and there is not enough glucose or sugar in the bloodstream, fat is released from fat cells and travels in the blood to the liver. The liver processes the fat into ketones. Ketones are released into the bloodstream to provide fuel for the body and increase the body's metabolism. Ketones are formed under conditions of starvation, fasting, or a diet low in carbohydrates.

To reach ketosis, you have to reduce your carbohydrates to less than 50 grams a day. Your consumption of fat can amount to about 75% of your food and about 15% protein. It varies from one person to another, but you should be able to reach ketosis in 3–14 days with consistency.

When you use a high quantity of carbohydrates, the metabolism uses carbohydrates much of the time. You never get fat processed for burning. If you lower the number of carbohydrates available, your body must adapt to burning your fat.

Seven tips to get into ketosis.

1. Reduce your consumption of carbs to 25–50 net carbs per day.
2. Comprise coconut oil into your diet.
3. Enhance your physical activity.
4. Increase fats that are safe.
5. Short fasting times
6. Maintain the consumption of protein.
7. Test levels of ketones.

If you consider these Nutritional adjustments, you should always consult with your doctor. Keto is a shift in lifestyle. You change the way you eat. To succeed, you should be persistent and take long-term implications into consideration.

CHAPTER 3:

Focus On Women Over 50

Changes in Your Body After 50

There is a lot of changes in your physical body as you age, and it is not in your hands. And it is not due to any single factor. Many things are working behind the scenes like the lifestyle choices that you make daily or even your genetics. Some factors are genuinely not in your control, but others, like the choices you make, can be altered. So, the decisions you make can literally either make your health or break it.

Some of the changes that occur in a woman's body after the age of 50 are as follows:

Menopause

The most significant change is menopause, and there is no denying it. Menopause can drastically change the body of a woman. But as the term suggests, menopause does not pause anything but instead causes a shift towards a different hormonal scenario. Your body then learns to strike a new kind of balance after considering its present situation of hormones. But what is more of a rollercoaster ride is not menopause itself but the symptoms that come before it. There are night sweats and hot flashes and drastic mood swings. Some women even face trouble sleeping, and some can even go into depression.

After menopause, women also face issues related to urinary incontinence, which is because their muscles in the pelvic region start weakening. Some women face this problem, known as pelvic prolapse, which is a significant reason behind urinary incontinence. If you have had children or are obese, then your risk of urinary incontinence increases further. And the weight, in turn, also enhances the chances of developing fibroids in the uterus. These, in the years, can either shrink or develop into more giant tumors. Some of the symptoms that signify that you have fibroids in your uterus are pelvic fullness, frequent urination, painful intercourse, and heavy bleeding.

Reduction in Bone Density

Several studies have proved that osteoporosis is a problem present in greater frequencies in women than in women. It is a condition where your bone density becomes less, rendering your bones weak and thin. And thus, then tend to break very easily. Every one in two women in their 50 is likely to experience a reduction in their bone density. Also, after menopause, 30% of the bone mass in women is lost. Moreover, if a woman has early menopause, that can cause an even more significant amount of bone loss by the time they reach 55.

Whenever you are in your 50s or have got your menopause before that, then get a bone density test done. In case you are already in the risk category of being inflicted by a reduced bone density, you should get tested more. You must also know that certain medications are not particularly good for your bone density and might compromise it. So, getting tried is essential.

Loss of Muscles

After you aged 50, there is a gradual decrease in muscle mass, and some people think that this happens in men only. But this is not true. Loss of muscle mass is something that affects everyone, including women. And with this, there is a decrease in your physical strength as well. The best method to avoid this is by engaging in exercises that are all about strength training. It will neutralize the effect a bit. Or, you can practice doing squats and lunges twice or thrice a week in your house itself. There is another benefit that you will derive from these exercises, and that is, you will be able to regain a better sense of balance.

Weaker Joints

With age, your joints will start becoming more fragile, and this is not because of a reduction in bone density, but because the cartilage present around your joints begins to wear down. The effects of these are felt even more when you are over 50. You'll start developing arthritis and joint pain problems, and your posture is also gets affected. Avoid slouching because the more slouch, the more your body lays stress on your joints, and they become weaker. Moreover, you need to keep a check on your weight too. When your body weight increases, your body has to carry that extra weight around even when the joints are becoming weak, which becomes difficult.

Signs of Aging on Skin

One of the obvious signs of aging is seen on your skin. There will be spots and fine lines and also a bit of sagging. Even if you maintain your skin a lot, there will be some signs of aging that you cannot avoid. The symptoms will become worse, especially if you were not caring about your skin during your younger years. You might have skipped sunscreen then, but now, doing that will wreak havoc on your skin. Moreover, your skin will get irritated very quickly, and, in some women, it also feels very dry.

The best way to deal with all these changes is to go for regular health screenings to be aware of what is happening in your body.

Menopause and Keto Diet

A woman that uses up such a multitude of carbohydrates can begin menopause indications. Exactly how about we watch how a ketogenic diet plan can assist with the signs and negative effects of this menopause.

Controlling Insulin Levels

By taking place a ketogenic diet plan, females with PCOS (polycystic-over-the-air problem) can help prevent their hormones. Exploration concentrated on the impact of low-glycemic diet plans has shown this influence. PCOS causes insulin affectability fears, to be aided by insulin-decreasing homes of low-glycemic carbohydrates.

Fat loss

Menopause can trigger metabolic treatment to alter and also reduce. One of the most widely known complaints of menopause is an increase in body weight and belly fat. A reduced level of estrogen commonly causes weight gain. A diet plan with virtually no carbohydrates is beneficial for decreasing muscle to fat ratio. Ketosis reduces hunger by controlling the development of the 'food cravings hormonal agent' called ghrelin. You are much less ravenous while in ketosis.

A decrease in Hot Flashes

No person extensively comprehends hot flashes, as well as why they happen. Hormonal adjustments that affect the command post, in all probability, have something to do with this. The switchboard deals with the internal heat's degree. Adjustments in hormonal representatives can also disrupt this indoor regulatory authority. It winds up being significantly sensitive to adjustments in interior warm level levels.

Ketones, in which its creation stimulates all through a ketogenic diet, make a solid wellspring of energy for the mind. Scientists have shown that ketones demo to support the nerve center. The body will handle its temperature degree much better. The proximity of ketones attempts to improve your body's indoor regulator.

Excellent Night's rest

You will enhance lay while on a ketogenic diet on account of a great deal steadier sugar degree. With substantially increasingly modified hormones and also significantly fewer warm flashes, you will relax much better. Reduced pressure and boosted success are 2 of the advantages of better rest.

CHAPTER 4:

Following The Keto Diet

What to Eat on a Keto Diet

Fats and Oils

Because fats will be included as part of all of your meals, we recommend that you choose the highest quality ingredients that you can afford. Some of your best choices for fat are:

- Ghee or clarified butter
- Avocado
- Coconut Oil
- Red Palm Oil
- Butter
- Coconut Butter
- Peanut Butter
- Chicken Fat
- Beef Tallow
- Non-hydrogenated Lard
- Macadamias and other nuts
- Egg Yolks
- Fish rich in Omega-3 Fatty Acids like salmon, mackerel, trout, tuna, and shellfish.

Protein

Those on a keto diet will generally keep fat intake high, carbohydrate intake low, and protein intake moderate. Those who are on a keto diet for weight loss have better success with higher protein and lower fat intake.

- Fresh meat: beef, veal, lamb, chicken, duck, pheasant, pork, etc.
- Deli meats: bacon, sausage, ham (make sure to watch out for added sugar and other fillers)
- Eggs: preferably free-range or organic eggs
- Fish: wild-caught salmon, catfish, halibut, trout, tuna, etc.
- Other seafood: lobster, crab, oyster, clams, mussels, etc.
- Peanut Butter: this is a great source of Protein, but choose a brand with no added Sugar

Dairy

Compared to other weight-loss diets, the keto diet encourages you to choose dairy products that are full fat. Some of the best dairy products that you can choose are:

- Hard and soft cheese: cream cheese, mozzarella, cheddar, etc.
- Cottage cheese
- Heavy whipping cream
- Sour cream
- Full-Fat yogurt

Vegetables

Overall, vegetables are rich in vitamins and minerals that contribute to a healthy body. However, if you're aiming to avoid carbs, you should limit starchy vegetables such as potatoes, yams, peas, corn, beans, and most legumes. Other vegetables that are high in carbohydrates, such as parsnips and squash, should also be limited. Instead, stick with green leafy vegetables and other low-carb veggies. Choose local or organic varieties if it's within your budget.

- Spinach
- Lettuce
- Collard greens
- Mustard greens
- Bok choy
- Kale
- Alfalfa sprouts
- Celery
- Tomato
- Broccoli
- Cauliflower

Fruits

Your choice of fruit on the keto diet is typically restricted to avocado and berries because fruits are high in carbohydrates and Sugar.

Drinks

- Water
- Black coffee
- Herbal tea
- Wine: white wine and dry red wine are okay only when consumed occasionally

Others

- Homemade mayo. When consuming store-bought mayo, watch out for added sugar.
- Homemade mustard
- Any type of spices or herbs
- Stevia and other non-nutritive sweeteners such as Swerve
- Sugar-free ketchup
- Dark chocolate/cocoa

What Foods to Avoid

1. Bread and Grains

Bread is a staple food in many countries. You have loaves, bagels, tortillas, and the list goes on. However, no matter what form bread takes, they still pack a lot of carbs. The same applies to whole-grain as well because they are made from refined flour. Depending on your daily carb limit, eating a sandwich or bagel can put make you go over your limit. So if you want to eat bread, it is best to make keto variants at home instead. Grains such as rice, wheat, and oats pack a lot of carbs as well. So limit or avoid that as well.

2. Fruits

Fruits are healthy for you. They could lower the risk of having heart diseases and cancer. However, there are a few that you need to avoid in your keto diet. Some fruits, such as bananas, raisins, dates, mango, and pear, pack quite a lot of carbs. As a general rule, avoid sweet and dried fruits. Berries are an exception because they do not contain as much sugar and are rich in Fiber. So you can still eat around 50 grams of them. Moderation is key.

3. Vegetables

Vegetables are just as healthy for your body. Most of the keto diet does not care how many vegetables you eat as long as they are low in starch. Vegetables that are high in Fiber can aid with weight loss. For one, they make you feel full for longer, so they help suppress your appetite. Another benefit is that your body would burn more calories to break and digest them.

Moreover, they help control blood sugar and aid with bowel movements. But that also means you need to avoid or limit vegetables that are high in starch because they have more carbs than fiber. That includes corn, potato, sweet potato, and beets.

4. Pasta

Pasta is also a staple food in many countries. It is versatile and convenient. As with any other suitable food, pasta is rich in carbs. So when you are on your keto diet, spaghetti, or many different types of pasta are not recommended. Thankfully, that does not mean you need to give up on it altogether. If you are craving pasta, you can try some other alternatives that are low in carbs such as spiralized veggies or shirataki noodles.

5. Cereal

Cereal is also a massive offender because Sugary breakfast cereals pack a lot of carbs. That also applies to "healthy cereals." Just because they use other words to describe their product does not mean that you should believe them. That also applies to oatmeal, whole-grain cereals, etc. So eating cereals when you are doing keto will make you go over your carb limit, and we haven't even added milk into the equation! Therefore, avoid whole-grain cereal or cereals altogether.

Know Your Macros

Every self-respecting diet must explain to the reader what macronutrients our body needs, how to calculate them, and how to manage them in the best possible way. There is no perfect diet; each of us is unique and different. We must learn to manage our diet completely independently. There are three macronutrients: carbohydrates, proteins, and fats.

Macronutrients are found in every food. They are the nutrients that fuel the body. Carbohydrates, proteins, and fats are included in the calories consumed and should be tracked while on the keto diet. The information needed is on the Nutritional value label found on foods. Accurately measure individual portions to be sure to have accurate Nutritional information. These nutrients being tracked are typically called "macros," a shortened version of the word macronutrient. By making adjustments to the SKD and HPKD, a gentler keto plan may be created to fit the needs of women over 50. First, we will look at the carbohydrates. You will be counting net carbs. Grams of net carbs are determined by subtracting the grams of dietary fiber and the grams of sugar alcohols from the grams of total carbohydrates. dietary fiber does not release insulin into the body. The same is true of sugar alcohols. As a result, you will be able to eat more Nutritionally, dense foods. You may satisfy your food cravings and hunger.

Next, we will look at fats. You will be eating 60 to 75% of your food as fat. This allows for a wide variety of foods, like bacon and pork rinds, to be included in your diet. Avocado, nuts, and other foods will be included in your diet as well. Because you will be eating food that is not processed, it will be important to eat healthy fats, including oil derived from natural food sources like avocado oil and coconut oil. High-quality butter and ghee will also be good sources of fat.

When we start to consider proteins, proteins do not need to be lean meats. The proteins included in Keto should not be lean but should be high in fat so that you consume appropriate amounts of fat. The keto diet is only effective when there is a high amount of fat consumed.

Now, let's start calculating the macros. To calculate the grams of net carbohydrates to include in your daily diet, it is important to determine your body weight and then your percentage of body fat. To do this, weigh yourself. After determining your weight, divide your body weight by your height in inches and square height in inches squared. Multiply that by 703, and you will have your BMI, or body mass index.

Lbs./height in inches, squared, times 703=BMI. So, in actuality, if you are a 5-foot 6-inch woman weighing 200 lbs. that's $200/66^2$ x 703=32.28. The BMI is 32.28.

Then calculate your body fat percentage. (1.2 x BMI) + (.23 * age) - 5.4 equals body fat percentage. When we plug in the BMI from our female example, (1.2 * 32.28) + (.23*55) - 5.4 =45.98

So, the body fat percentage is 45.98%. Now that you have your body fat percentage, take your body fat percentage and multiply it by your body weight. 45.98% x 200 lb. That equals 91.96 lbs. of body fat. Subtract the body fat from your weight, and you have your LBM (Lean Body Mass). So, 200 - 91.96 equals 108.04. The LBM is 108.04.

Now, it's time to determine the number of macronutrients to eat each day.

We can start with the calculation for protein. There are .8 grams per pound of lean body mass. In our example, .8* 108.04 equals 84 grams. This is equal to 346 calories because there are four calories in each gram of protein. In our example, 20% of the calories the daily calories will be from protein. Therefore, 346 calories/.20 equals 1730 calories per day.

The total calories are 1730 calories per day.

To determine the number of carbohydrates, let's look at the number of carbohydrates in a gentler keto. 10% of the daily calories will come from carbs. 10% of 1730 calories is 173 calories. If you divide 173 calories by 4 (there are four calories in each carbohydrate), you will have 43.25g of carbohydrates as your daily allowance.

The remaining calories for each day will be fat:

346 Calories, Protein 86.50g 20%

+173 Calories, Carbohydrate 43.25g 10%

519 calories of protein and carbs

-1730 (Total Daily Calories)

1211 Calories, fat 134.56g 70%

There are nine calories in each fat gram. 1,211 Calories/9 calories = 134.56g of fat for each day, or 70% of your daily calorie intake.

These macros will change as your BMI and LBM change. Make sure you adjust your macros every four or five weeks while you're losing weight so that your macros are accurate. You will want to record what you are eating and review your success in weight loss. This will allow you to track how your body is reacting to food combinations. Each body is different. It is important to see how you feel when you are eating different foods and combinations of foods as your approach ketosis. Be sure you're eating whole grains and getting Fiber through leafy green vegetables. You will also want to be very familiar with Nutrition labels to ensure you're not consuming hidden carbohydrates without realizing you are doing so.

What's Keto Flu?

Keto flu is a symptom set that certain people encounter when they first start their keto diet. These signs, similar to flu, are caused by the transition of the body to a new diet with few carbs. Decreasing your carb intake enhances your body to burn ketones rather than glucose for energy. Ketones are by-products of a breakup of fat and, after a ketogenic diet, become the primary source of fuel. fat is usually reserved for use as a secondary source of fuel when glucose is not accessible.

This turns to energy-burning fat in ketosis. It happens in certain conditions, including hunger and fasting. Ketosis can, however, also be accomplished by a very low-carb diet. Carbohydrates are usually reduced to less than 50 grams a day in a ketogenic diet. This drastic drop can cause a shock to the body, and symptoms similar to those when a dangerous drug like caffeine is weaned.

Keto flu is a term used to characterize flu-like symptoms due to the start of a deficient carbs ketogenic diet.

Symptoms

Switching to a very low carbs diet is a significant shift, so it may take time for your body to adapt to this new diet. This transition phase can be challenging for some people. Signs of keto flu may be seen during the first few days of carbohydrate cutting. The symptoms can vary from mild to vary and severe between individuals.

Although some may shift to a ketogenic diet without side effects, others may experience a symptom or more:

- Vomiting
- Nausea
- Diarrhea
- Constipation
- Irritability
- Headache
- Muscle cramps
- Weakness
- Poor concentration
- Dizziness
- Difficulty sleeping
- Stomach pain
- Sugar cravings
- Muscle soreness

These symptoms are typically reported by people who just began their ketogenic diet and can be disturbing. Symptoms usually last about one week, but some people can have them for a long time, however, there are ways to reduce them.

Many people may experience signs such as diarrhea, Fatigue, aches, and pain when starting a ketogenic diet.

How to Get Rid of Keto Flu

The flu keto will make you feel wretched. Fortunately, there is a way to reduce its flu-like symptoms and to make the adjustment process easier for your body.

Stay hydrated

To maintain optimum health, drinking enough water is essential and can also help to minimize symptoms. You can easily dump water in a keto diet, which raises the risk of dehydration. Glycogen, the stored carbohydrate shape, binds to the body's water. When Dietary carbohydrates are decreased, the amount of glycogen falls, and water is excreted. Hydration may lead to symptoms such as Fatigue and muscle cramping. Fluid replacement is particularly necessary when you have keto-flu-related diarrhea that can lead to further fluid losses.

Avoid strenuous exercise

While exercise is vital for maintaining good health and managing body weight, exercises in the case of keto flu symptoms should be avoided. Fatigue, muscle cramps, and stomach pain in the first week of a ketogenic diet are normal so that you can rest your body. Activities like heavy walking, hiking, weightlifting, and challenging training may need to be put on the rear burner as the system is adapted to new fuels.

Although such workouts should be avoided if you experience keto flu, light activities such as walking, yoga, or cycling may improve symptoms.

Swap electrolytes

The replacement of dietary electrolytes may lead to reducing keto-flu symptoms. If insulin levels, an important hormone that helps the body absorb glucose from the bloodstream, decrease after a ketogenic diet. If insulin levels decline, excess Sodium is released from the kidneys from the body. Moreover, the keto diet limits many potassium foods, including beans, fruit, and starchy vegetables. Adequate quantities of these essential nutrients are an excellent way to achieve control during the diet's adaptation phase.

Salting food to taste and using ketos high in potassium, such as green leafy vegetables and avocados, is an excellent way to guarantee a balanced electrolyte balance. These foods also contain high levels of magnesium that can alleviate muscle cramps, sleep, and headaches.

Get enough sleep

Tiredness and irritability are typical symptoms of individuals who adhere to a ketogenic diet. The lack of sleep causes stress hormone cortisol levels to increase in the body that can adversely influence the mood and worsen the symptoms of keto-flu.

If you have a hard time falling or sleeping, try one of the following tips:

- Minimize the consumption of caffeine: Caffeine is a sleep-induced stimulant. If you want to drink caffeinated drinks, do so only in the morning, in order not to disturb your sleep.
- Eliminate ambient light: Cut mobile phones, computers, and TVs off into the bedroom to create a dark and restful sleep.
- Take a shower: The addition of Epsom salt or essential lavender oil to your bath is a safe way to relax and sleep.
- Wake up early: Waking regularly concurrently and sleep avoidance will help normalize your sleep habits and increase your sleep quality over time.

Ensure that you eat enough carbs (and fat)

If you move to a low-carb diet, you may want foods restricted to the ketogenic diet, such as bread, cookies, bagels, and pasta. But eating enough Fat, the primary source of food in the ketogenic diet, eliminates your cravings and keeps you happy.

Research actually shows that low-carb diets help minimize sweets and high-carb food cravings. Many with a hard time adjusting to the ketogenic diet may need to gradually, rather than at once, remove carbohydrates. A gradual cut back on carbs while growing your diet's fat and protein will help to ease the transition and minimize symptoms of keto-flu. You can regulate the keto influenza by keeping it hydrated, substituting electrolytes, sleeping a lot, avoiding challenging tasks, consuming enough Fat, and slowly slicing carbs.

Why Do Some People Have Keto Flu?

People respond differently to ketogenic diets. Some will have keto-flu symptoms for weeks, while others may adapt to the new diet with no adverse side effects. The symptoms of people are related to how their bodies respond to a new source of fuel. carbs typically provide the body with glucose energy.

Those who eat many carbs, especially refined carbs such as pasta, cereal, and soda, may have a more challenging time when they start their ketogenic diets.

Thus, adjustment to an excessively Fat, low-carb diet can be a challenge for others, although others have little or no keto-flu symptoms between fuel sources.

Some people respond quickly to ketogenic diets than others are unaware of, but the driving factors behind keto grip are expected to be biology, electrolyte depletion, dehydration, and carbohydrate withdrawal.

How Long Is It Going to Last?

Fortunately, for most people, the painful effects of keto flu last just about a week. However, it is more difficult for some people to adapt to this high-fat, low-carb diet. Symptoms may last for several weeks for these individuals. Fortunately, as the body gets used to burning ketones into energy, these symptoms can eventually decrease. Though keto-flu symptoms are generally recorded by people who switch to ketogenic diets, it is best to contact your doctor and rule out other reasons if you are especially unwell and suffer from symptoms like severe diarrhea, fever, or vomiting.

Some individuals may experience symptoms of keto-flu due to genetics, loss of electrolytes, drying, and removal of carbohydrates. The keto influenza lasts typically for about a week, although some symptoms may last over a month.

How to Test Ketone Levels

When you are first starting the ketogenic diet, you will want to choose a method for testing your ketone levels. As you follow the diet more, you will be able to tell if you are in ketosis through the signs and symptoms, but we all have to start somewhere! Luckily for you, there are several different methods to test ketone levels, including urine, breath, and blood. I suggest the blood method, as it is typically the most accurate representation.

On that note, for true beginners, the urine test for ketones may be enough. In the beginning stages, your body is still learning how to use this new fuel. During this time, your body will be filtering quite a bit through your urine, so you will easily be able to tell if your body is producing ketones with a simple test. Over time, your body will adapt, and you will begin to lose fewer ketones through your urine because your body is utilizing them properly.

While following the ketogenic diet, your ketone levels will be anywhere from 0 to 3, and sometimes higher. These ketones are measured in millimoles per liter or mmol/L. You will want to check your general ranges to make sure you are in ketosis and following the diet properly. This is important to know because sometimes, carbs can creep up on you and ruin your process without you even realizing it!

Urine Ketone Testing

The first method we will discuss is the urine ketone testing method. This method requires you to pee on a urine strip, which will change colors. These can be a good method as they are fairly affordable, and you will be able to find them at most pharmacies. The downfall of this method is that they aren't always reliable, especially after you've been following the ketogenic diet for a while.

Blood Ketone Testing

This method of testing for ketones is done by a blood glucose meter. This device is a pen that you press into your fingertip to draw a very small blood sample. Once you have your sample, you will apply it to a test strip to monitor your blood ketone levels. This is an excellent method (if you don't mind needles) as it is very accurate. However, it should be noted that this method is a bit expensive. Generally, it will cost you anywhere from $5–$10 per strip.

Breath Ketone Testing

Finally, we have the Ketonix breath meter. This device works by measuring the amount of acetone that it detects on your breath. While this is a more affordable option, it isn't always the most reliable. Much like with the urine testing, there are several factors that can change the results, and your body will be releasing less ketones in your breath and urine as it learns to use them as fuel.

CHAPTER 5:

Important Tips for Success with The Ketogenic Diet

Remember, the keto diet is more than an eating plan; it's a whole new lifestyle. If you want to stick with this diet for the long term, here are some pointers to keep in mind:

Consider your motivation for starting the keto diet

If you want to make this diet plan part of your life, you need to make sure you're doing it for the right reasons. If you're just starting the diet to join the trend, chances are, you might give up at the first sign of difficulty. However, if you have a good reason to follow the diet and you're sure that it will motivate you, then there's a good chance you will follow through. Some of the common reasons why people start this diet include the following:

Incorporating the diet as part of the treatment plan for certain conditions. For instance, inflammation, diabetes, heart disease, brain-related disorders, and even cancer.

To lose weight, especially for those who have a hard time losing fat.

To achieve and stay in a state of ketosis.

Learn how to count your macros

This is especially important at the start of your journey. As time goes by, you will learn how to estimate your meals without having to use a food scale.

Prepare your kitchen for your keto-friendly foods

Once you've made the choice, it's time to get rid of all the foods in your kitchen that aren't allowed in the keto diet. To do this, check the Nutritional labels of all the food items. Of course, there's no need to throw everything away. You can donate foods you don't need to food kitchens and other institutions that give food to the needy.

Purchase some keto strips for yourself

These are important so you can check your ketone levels and track your progress. You can purchase keto strips in pharmacies and online. For instance, some of the best keto strips available on Amazon are Perfect Keto Ketone Test Strips, SmackFat Ketone Strips, and One Earth Ketone Strips.

These are important for beginners, but if you have already been following the diet for some time, you will learn how to determine when your body is in ketosis just by how you're feeling.

Download a keto diet app to help you with your journey

These days, there are apps for everything! If you need to find more motivation to keep you on the path to a keto lifestyle, you can download an app for yourself. There are plenty of apps available, and they all have their own features. Research about these apps to find out which app would be the best one for you.

Here are a few great keto apps you can try:

- MyFitnessPal: This app has more than 150 million registered users now. It's one of the most popular apps out there, and it also has its own website. With this app, you can keep track of your macros and determine your best nutrient and calorie intake based on your own personal health goals.
- Keto Diet: You can think of this app as your own personal keto sidekick. Use it to keep track of your weight as well as your macros. With it, you can find out how the changes you're making in your diet are affecting your body.
- Carb Manager: This is another excellent keto companion as it has a database of over a million foods along with their macronutrient, micronutrient, and net carbohydrate information. Using this app makes it easier for you to shop for the foods to incorporate into your daily meals.

Ask your doctor if you need to take supplements

Whether you're completely healthy or have an existing medical condition, it's important to speak with your doctor first before you start. That way, you can learn more about the diet, ask any questions, and look for recommendations for supplements you can take to complement your keto diet.

Find an Activity You Enjoy

When you have done enough exercise, you will know what activities you like. One way to encourage yourself to exercise more regularly is by making it entertaining than a chore. If possible, stick to your favorite activities, and you can get the most out of your exercises. Keep in mind that the activities you enjoy may not be effective or needed, so you need to find other exercises to compensate for, which you may not enjoy. For instance, if you like jogging, you can work your leg muscles, but your arms are not involved. So, you need to do pushups or other strength training exercises.

Hydrate Properly

That means drinking enough water or herbal tea and ditching sweetened beverages or other drinks that contain sugar altogether. Making the transition will be difficult for the first few weeks, but your body will be thanking you for it. There is nothing healthier than good old plain water, and the recommended amount is 2 gallons a day.

Get Enough Sleep

Getting enough sleep helps your body regulate the hormones in your body, so try to aim for 7 to 9 hours of sleep a day. You can get more restful sleep by creating a nighttime routine that involves not looking at a computer, phone, or TV screen for at least 1 hour before bed. You can drink warm milk or water to help your body relax or even do 10 to 20 minutes of stretching to get a restful sleep.

Have the proper mindset

Your mindset is one of the most important things you need to change when you've decided to follow the keto lifestyle. Without the right mindset, you might not stick with the diet long enough to enjoy all its benefits. Also, the proper mindset will keep you motivated to keep going no matter what challenges come your way. Here are some tips to help you achieve the proper mindset to achieve success:

Think of your motivation or the reasons why you want to start the keto diet. If you think it will help, list out these reasons and refer back to them when you're feeling challenged.

Make a list of your health goals—both the simple ones that are easily achievable and the significant ones that require more time and effort.

Do a lot of research to learn about the keto diet so you know exactly how you will approach this new lifestyle.

CHAPTER 6:

Why Is the Regular Ketogenic Diet Not Recommended for Women Over 50?

Getting to the age of 50 means many psychological and physical changes in women such as hormonal problems, menopause, irritability, inflammation, lethargy, weak muscles and bones, and so on. Also, some women develop diabetes, Alzheimer's, and cardiovascular problems.

The Keto diet not only helps you attain your weight loss goal but is also beneficial for stabilizing insulin levels, suppressing your appetite, fueling cognitive power, and balancing hormonal levels, especially after menopause. Instead of following other fad diets claiming instant weight loss, adopt a healthy, tailored Keto diet for women over 50.

Why a normal keto diet is not recommended for women over 50

You cut your carbs down to minimum levels, i.e. less than 15 grams with a normal Keto diet. Cutting down carbs severely and suddenly is bad for you, because of aging your metabolism decreases by 25%, and with every passing year, your bones and muscles increasingly become weaker.

We also become more vulnerable to many physiological and psychological diseases, such as cardiovascular disease, obesity, Alzheimer's, or diabetes. Adopting a regular Keto diet plan can lead to many side effects, such as;

- Headaches
- Dizziness
- Fatigue

- Brain fog and difficulty focusing
- Lack of motivation and irritability
- Nausea
- Keto flu
- Inflammation
- And more...

These side effects cause many women to pull back and lose hope. It's all because you haven't been told about the likely side effects that you can suffer if you dive headfirst into the Keto diet. However, by consuming the right amount of fats while eating as much as you want within the range of the specific foods presented in this book, you will get your desired results.

For this, you need a specific Keto diet plan which will not only benefit you via weight loss but will also help build muscles, stabilize your blood sugar levels, and maximize your energy levels. And for all this, the Keto diet for women over 50 is a perfect option for you.

CHAPTER 7:

The Most Common Mistakes and How to Avoid Them

Do you feel like you are giving your all to the keto diet but you still aren't seeing the results you want? You are measuring ketones, working out, and counting your macros, but you still aren't losing the weight you want. Here are the most common mistakes that most people make when beginning the keto diet.

Too Many Snacks

There are many snacks you can enjoy while following the keto diet, like nuts, avocado, seeds, and cheese. But snacking can be an easy way to get too many calories into the diet while giving your body an easy fuel source besides stored fat. Snacks need to be only used if you frequently hunger between meals. If you aren't extremely hungry, let your body turn to your stored fat for its fuel between meals instead of dietary fat.

Not Consuming Enough fat

The ketogenic diet isn't all about low carbs. It's also about high fats. You need to be getting about 75 percent of your calories from healthy fats, five percent from carbs, and 20 percent from protein. fat makes you feel fuller longer, so if you eat the correct amount, you will minimize your carb cravings, and this will help you stay in ketosis. This will help your body burn fat faster.

Consuming Excessive calories

You may hear people say you can eat what you want on the keto diet as long as it is high in fat. Even though we want that to be true, it is very misleading. Healthy fats need to make up the biggest part of your diet. If you eat more calories than what you are burning, you will gain weight, no matter what you eat because these excess calories get stored as fat. An average adult only needs about 2,000 calories each day, but this will vary based on many factors like activity level, height, and gender.

Consuming A Lot of Dairies

For many people, dairy can cause inflammation and keep them from losing weight. Dairy is a combo food meaning it has carbs, protein, and fats. If you eat a lot of cheese as a snack for the fat content, you are also getting a dose of carbs and protein with that fat. Many people can tolerate dairy, but moderation is the key. Stick with no more than one to two ounces of cheese or cream at each meal. Remember to factor in the protein content.

Consuming A Lot of protein

The biggest mistake that most people make when just beginning the keto diet is consuming too much protein. Excess protein gets converted into glucose in the body called gluconeogenesis. This is a natural process where the body converts the energy from fats and proteins into glucose when glucose isn't available. When following a ketogenic diet, gluconeogenesis happens at different rates to keep body function. Our bodies don't need a lot of carbs, but we do need glucose. You can eat absolute zero carbs, and through gluconeogenesis, your body will convert other substances into glucose to be used as fuel.

This is why carbs only make up five percent of your macros. Some parts of our bodies need carbs to survive, like kidneys, medulla, and red blood cells. With gluconeogenesis, our bodies make and stores extra glucose as glycogen just in case supplies become too low.

In a normal diet, when carbs are always available, gluconeogenesis happens slowly because the need for glucose is extremely low. Our body runs on glucose and will store excess protein and carbs as fat.

It does take time for our bodies to switch from using glucose to burning fats. Once you are in ketosis, your body will use fat as the main fuel source and will start to store excess protein as glycogen.

Not Getting Enough Water

Water is crucial for your body. Water is needed for all your body does, and this includes burning fat. If you don't drink enough water, it can cause your metabolism to slow down, and this can halt your weight loss. Drinking 64 ounces or one-half gallon every day will help your body burn fat, flush out toxins, and circulate nutrients. When you are just beginning the keto diet, you might need to drink more water since your body will begin to get rid of body fat by flushing it out through urine.

Consuming Too Many Sweets

Some people might indulge in keto brownies and keto cookies that are full of sugar substitutes just because their net carb content is low, but you have to remember that you are still eating calories. Eating sweets might increase your carb cravings. Keto sweets are great on occasion; they don't need to be a staple in the diet.

Not Getting Enough Sleep

Getting plenty of sleep is needed in order to lose weight effectively. Without the right amount of sleep, your body will feel stressed, and this could result in your metabolism slowing down. It might cause it to store fat instead of burning fat. When you feel tired, you are more tempted to drink more lattes for energy, eat a snack to give you an extra boost, or order takeout rather than cooking a healthy meal. Try to get between seven and nine hours of sleep each night. Understand that your body uses that time to burn fat without you even lifting a finger.

Low on Electrolytes

Most people will experience the keto flu when they begin this diet. This happens for two reasons when your body changes from burning carbs to burning fat, your brain might not have enough energy, and this, in turn, can cause grogginess, headaches, and nausea. You could be dehydrated, and your electrolytes might be low since the keto diet causes you to urinate often.

Getting the keto flu is a great sign that you are heading in the right direction. You can lessen these symptoms by drinking more water or taking supplements that will balance your electrolytes.

Consuming Hidden carbs

Many foods look like they are low carb, but they aren't. You can find carbs in salad dressings, sauces, and condiments. Be sure to check Nutrition labels before you try new foods to make sure it doesn't have any hidden sugar or carbs. It just takes a few seconds to skim the label, and it might be the difference between whether or not you'll lose weight. If you have successfully ruled out all of the above, but you still aren't losing weight, you might need to talk with your doctor to make sure you don't have any health problems that could be preventing your weight loss. This can be frustrating, but stick with it, stay positive, and stay in the game. When the keto diet is done correctly, it is one of the best ways to lose weight.

CHAPTER 8:

Intermittent Fasting and Super Foods

Intermittent Fasting

Intermittent fasting is fasting when you keep away any foodstuff involving calories among ordinary nutritious Ingredients. It is not starvation or a way for you to eat junk food with no consequences. There are various methods used to practice IF; they divide time into hours or divide time into days. Since the regiment's response varies from person to person, no process can be called the best.

Knowing that intermittent fasting cannot make you lose the additional pounds you may have instantaneously is essential, but it can help you prevent unhealthy addictions to meals. It's a Nutritional practice that requires you to be determined to follow to get the maximum gain. If you already have a minimum duration to eat due to your schedule, this regiment will suit you like a duck to water, but you will always need to be conscious of what you are eating if you are a foodie. Choose the appropriate regiment after expert guidance. You should see it as a segment of your schedule to get healthy, but not the only component.

Intermittent fasting is for those who want to regulate their hormones and burn surplus body fat. This diet allows for healthier whole foods and an all-round diet, which is better than living off processed foods and Sugars, which are unhealthy. It can also benefit individuals who are Sugar-addicted or those who ate empty calories. Drinks and sodas with very few nutrients, but full of Calories, are included in these products. Finally, people generally want to do better in life and enjoy a food plan that doesn't require too much planning or maintenance.

Health Benefits of Intermittent Fasting

According to research, an intermittent fasting diet does more than just burn fat. This metabolic change affects your brain and body. There are numerous health benefits of practicing intermittent fasting, including a long and healthy life, a sharp mind, and a lean body. Many changes happen when you do intermittent fasting, which protects your organs from chronic diseases such as heart disease, type 2 diabetes, some neurodegenerative disorders, many cancers, and inflammatory diseases. Different variations in intermittent fasting diet plans show pretty fantastic health benefits. Research has backed up this belief that it might have various positive effects, ranging from weight loss and a healthier body to a low risk of numerous diseases and a prolonged lifespan. But, fasting usually is not advisable for children, people having severe health issues, and pregnant women. Here are given some amazing benefits of intermittent fasting that research has approved so far:

Improvement in Brain and Memory Function

According to research, intermittent fasting helps in boosting memory performance in animals as well as in adult humans. This eating pattern also improves brain function. It helps in combating diseases like Alzheimer's. As per another study, intermittent fasting also enhances the cognitive function, neuroplasticity, which structures the ability of your brain to rebuild and reorganize itself, and the overall improvement in the brain functions.

Better Endurance Level

Intermittent fasting helps in fat loss and maintains muscle mass. It improves physical performance and enhances the endurance levels. Research done on mice has shown positive results in these aspects. It also improves the health of our tissues in the long term. The growth hormone also shows increased levels as a result of intermittent fasting. Which ultimately helps in improving metabolism and body composition.

Control Diabetes

Adult humans having obesity can lose weight by adopting an effective intermittent fasting plan which ultimately controls diabetes as it helps in significantly decreasing and controlling the levels of blood sugar. In recent times, intermittent fasting has become novel and one of the most effective ways to treat type 2, diabetes patients. There are many reports of cases where patients lost weight and also witnessed improved blood sugar levels. They did not have to take diabetes medications, and the disease appeared less harmful. But more research is needed to prove this approach as safe and useful in the long term as intermittent fasting demands a significant change in eating habits. Not many people can stick to that in the long term.

Improved Heart Health

The positive changes in intermittent fasting lower Cholesterol levels. Intermittent fasting improves blood pressure. It maintains and keeps the heart rate in balance. It keeps the risk factors in control that may cause heart-related issues and disease. According to the studies, when the insulin levels in your blood fall, the risk of serious cardiovascular events like heart failure will also fall. It is crucial for type 2 diabetes patients. These patients are at risk of heart diseases 2–4 times more than people without diabetes. Observational research has also shown that intermittent fasting delivers both metabolic and cardiovascular benefits. It is noteworthy that changes in metabolic parameters like lower levels of blood sugar and triglycerides happen because of weight loss, and intermittent fasting can help you achieve that.

Decrease Inflammation

Research has found that intermittent fasting patterns of eating reduce certain blood markers that can cause inflammation. According to research, intermittent fasting kick-start releases cells named monocytes, which are immune cells related to high inflammation that can lead to severe damage to the tissues. Its population has been increasing the blood circulation of the body because of unhealthy eating habits people have adopted in recent years. These cells usually go into sleep mode in fasting periods. They become less inflammatory in their effects than those cells which have been fed. According to researchers, monocytes significantly decrease in numbers after fasting, and that is the strong link between inflammatory disease and high-calorie diet patterns. Considering the number of illnesses caused by chronic inflammation, there should be an enormous investigation of the effects of fasting on anti-inflammation because many people are being affected by this.

Effective in Cancer Treatment

Although there has not been much research on the possible relationship between intermittent fasting and cancer, early reports suggest positive results. The study conducted on cancer patients has suggested that the consequences of chemotherapy might be eliminated by having a fast before treatment. It has also been supported by other studies where the cancer patients had the alternate day fast. Their fasting approach before chemotherapy treatment resulted in positive cure rates. So, the comprehensive analysis of cancer and fasting has supported the argument that fasting reduces cancer risk and various cardiovascular diseases. Intermittent fasting has a considerable potential for prevention and also the treatment of cancer. As we know, intermittent fasting reduces glucose and insulin levels, increases Ketone body and anti-inflammatory levels, so it can generate a large protective environment to reduce carcinogenesis and DNA damage. Thus, intermittent fasting not only protects you from cancer but also enhances the natural death of the pre-cancerous damaging cells. A study conducted on ten subjects having various malignancies showed that combining fasting with chemotherapy showed a decrease in commonly seen side effects of chemotherapy. The impact of fasting on the toxicity of chemotherapy and the progression of cancer is being studied in various clinical researches in the US and Europe.

Weight-loss

Most people trying intermittent fasting have gained positive results in cutting their weight. You may plan heavy meals, but eating them consistently is not an easy practice. Intermittent fasting is one of the useful options for someone who is looking forward to weight loss as it provides the most amazing and simple way to lose the overall calories without even changing your lifestyle that much. Also, if someone eats large portions for lunch and the evening meal, he/she will end up having fewer calorie intake than someone who has 3–4 regular meals. Cutting out meals in intermittent fasting works very well for losing weight.

When you try to decrease the calorie intake, losing weight is inevitable dramatically. But it will not do any good for you. It will cause many health problems for you, including severe muscle loss. When you go for intermittent fasting, the body moves towards a conservation mode that burns calories slowly. It is not the fat that the body burns at the early stages of fasting, it is the water or fluid. When you turn back to the eating period, any kind of lost weight will return quickly. Most people tend to regain the weight that they lost during fasting. They possibly add extra pounds just because gaining weight happens because of slower metabolism. So, it is crucial to practice the right approach and choose the one that goes for fat burning and more effective weight loss.

Detoxify Your Body

Intermittent fasting might be a stressful activity, and your body might take time to adjust to it. It might not immediately love the idea, but it will ultimately give you huge benefits. According to research, even occasional fast has a lot of benefits, and it has been proven with research that autophagy and intermittent fasting can cure cancer. It can make the treatment more productive and protect healthy cells while reducing the side effects of the treatment. The resting period involved in intermittent fasting enhances autophagy, a crucial function of your body to detoxify and clean out the dead and damaged cells. Giving your body a small break in digestion and constant eating gives your body a better place to heal itself. It helps in eliminating all the junk inside your body cells that might accelerate the aging process. A study found out that time-limited feeding, as we do in intermittent fasting, increases the expression of an autophagy gene and also a protein called mTOR that regulates cell growth. It has been done on 11 participants for four consecutive days. There has been another study that has shown that food limitation is a very well-recognized approach to boost autophagy that offers many protective benefits to your brain.

Training your body for autophagy will benefit you in the very long term. Autophagy refers to self-eating your body. It might sound scary, but it is one of the effective ways to cleanse the body. So, your body itself becomes your cleansing house. During this process, cells create many membranes to hunt down dead scraps, or diseased cells. Then it strips them into parts and utilizes the molecules to gain energy. It can also be helpful in making a new cell. It is your body's recycling program. Research has shown that autophagy plays a role in the immune response and inflammation. It acts as a perfect immune effector that mediates the pathogen clearance. Autophagy is the phenomenon of self-digestion that happens inside your body cells during intermittent fasting periods. It controls essential physiological functions that break down cellular components and then recycled them as well. Autophagy rapidly provides fuel to gain energy. It serves as a very strong base that leads to the renewal of the cellular components. Therefore, it plays a crucial part in cellular response and controls starvation and stress during fasting periods. Autophagy eliminates invading intracellular viruses and bacteria.

That is how it cleans your body. Your body cells use autophagy for the elimination of damaged organelles and Proteins. Through this mechanism, it counterattacks the negative results of aging.

Metabolic Syndrome and Intermittent Fasting

Intermittent fasting has the ability to reverse many metabolic syndromes as it enhances insulin sensitivity, balances blood pressure, and stimulates lipolysis. Reduced body Fat, balanced blood pressure, and glucose metabolism are some of the additional benefits of intermittent fasting. As per the research done on obese people in which they were studied for a 6-month period while on an intermittent fasting diet, consuming only 500 to 600 calorie intakes during fasting periods, showed abdominal fat-loss, improved sensitivity levels of insulin, and blood pressure.

Anti-aging

You will not find a lot of research on human bodies regarding intermittent fasting. Although some research done on animals suggests that it boosts lifespan and slows down the aging signs. Calorie restriction is the best and the most effective approach to combat aging. The traditional calorie restriction cuts down the calories by almost 20 to 40%, which is not the best option, and plan to do things that way. The recent research on animals and humans has shown many previously unknown mechanisms that are involved in anti-aging. There are some additional effects of intermittent fasting on human cells, which lead to the potential anti-aging phenomenon. It includes the mTOR pathway, ketogenesis, and autophagy.

Choosing intermittent fasting without suffering from malnutrition is the most efficient and consistent anti-aging intervention. It undoubtedly expands lifespan according to the research done on animals and some humans. The study found that the longevity biomarkers, i.e., body temperature and insulin level, and also the DNA damage decreased significantly in humans by prolonged intermittent fasting. Other mechanisms also prove the claim made by researchers in explaining the anti-aging effects by adopting intermittent fasting, including decreased lipid peroxidation, high efficiency of the oxidative repair, increased antioxidant defense system, and reduced mitochondrial generation rate.

Healthy Sleep Patterns

Our eating habits have a considerable impact on sleepiness and wakefulness. Some intermittent fasting believers have reported an improved sleeping pattern as a result of changing their eating patterns through fasting. Both intermittent fasting and mealtimes have a considerable impact on the quality of our sleep because they regulate the circadian rhythm that determines our sleep patterns. If you have a regulated and balanced circadian rhythm, you will fall asleep quite quickly. You will also feel refreshed when you wake up. There is another theory that states that having the last meal early will help you to digest the food way before going to the bed. Digestion works best when you are upright. Sleeping with a full stomach causes heartburn or acid reflux, which makes falling asleep really difficult.

Low-Calorie Intake in an Efficient Way

Following an approach like 16/8 intermittent fasting, you eat for just 8-hour a day. It helps in limiting the calorie intake level. Typically, people have more calorie intake than what is actually needed. One of the most efficient habits to remain healthy and stop fats from growing significantly in the body is by adopting the habit of exercising 4 to 5 days every week. It burns extra calories in the body. People eating a lot of fast foods take more calories and unhealthy nutrients in their diet. But intermittent fasting protects your body from storing that extra fat with having less calorie intake in the body.

Different Methods

IF regiments are numerous to the point that you can choose from any that you like. Always make sure to select a regiment that will fit in your schedule so that it is possible to maintain it.

There are several short methods for fasting, including:

The 12-hour fast

That's what the regular living routine is called as you eat three meals a day and fast at night as you sleep. The generally small breakfast would break the fast. It is called the traditional method. Any regiment can help you lose weight only if you follow it correctly.

The higher the levels of insulin are as a result of more people adding regular eating and snacking. It can cause resistance to insulin and, ultimately, obesity. This fasting technique sets aside twelve hours in which the body has low levels of insulin, reducing the likelihood of insulin resistance. It can't help you lose excess fat, but it can help prevent obesity.

The 16-hour fast

This fasting for 16 hours, followed by an 8-hour window where you can eat what you like. Luckily you can sleep through most of it, so it's not difficult to keep doing it. Because it requires only small changes like just skipping your lunch, it has an enormous advantage over others, such as the 12 hours fast.

The 20-hour fast

It's called the' warrior diet.' It includes fasting all day long and eating a lot of calories at night. It's meant to keep you from having breakfast, lunch, and other meals for most of the day, so you're getting all your nutrients from dinner. It is a division scheme of 20:4 with four hours of food followed by twenty hours of fasting. It's one of the easiest to do as you're allowed to eat a huge meal of calorific value, so you're going to feel fuller for longer. Start your daytime calories and have a big evening dinner to relax in this diet. You're going to gradually reduce what you're eating during the day and eventually leave dinner as your only dinner.

The longer you do these fasting regiments, the more you will be able to maintain a fast. You will come to find out that you will not always feel hungry. The excitement of benefits will make you increase your period of fasting by a couple of hours. Unknowingly, therefore, you are plunging into longer stages of fasting. You can adhere to your regiment religiously, but eating an extra hour will not ruin your fasting or fat burning.

The easiest way to track your feeding is to do it once a day is because it doesn't require a lot of thought. It's just eating at that moment every day on one dinner so that you can use your mental energy on the more important stuff. Unfortunately, it can cause a plateau of weight loss, where you are not losing or gaining weight. That's because you're going to consume the same number of calories every day and significantly less on a typical working day than you would eat. That's the best way to maintain your weight. You will have to change your fasting regimen to lose fat after a while. Timing your meals and fasting windows will lead to optimal loss of fat instead of random fasting. Choose one that can be maintained and modified if necessary.

There are longer fasting regiments, these include:

The 24-hour fast

It's a scheme of eating breakfast, lunch, or dinner in a day and then eating the following day at the same time. If you decide to eat lunch, then it only involves skipping breakfast and dinner, so nothing is disrupted in your life. It saves time and money because you're not going to eat as much, and piling up dishes will not be a worry of yours. Knowing that you are fasting will be a task for people unless they are very interested in eating methods. By eating unprocessed natural foods, you should have enough vitamins, minerals, and oxygen to avoid nutrient deficiencies. You can do this weekly, but twice or three times a week, it is suggested.

During such long fasts, you should not knowingly avoid eating calories. What you are taking should be high in fat, low in carbohydrates, and unprocessed; there's nothing you shouldn't eat. It would be best if you consumed until you are adequately fed as the duration of fasting lets you burn a bunch of Fat, and it will be difficult over time to try to cut more purposefully.

The 36-hour fast

You retain in this fast for one and a half days without eating. For instance, if you eat lunch today, you consume no meal until the day's breakfast after the following day. This fast should be done about three times a week for people with type 2 diabetes. After the person reaches the desired weight and all diabetes medications are successfully removed, they can reduce the number of days of fasting to a level that will make it easier for the person to do while maintaining their gains. The longer he's diabetes, the longer he's going to last. Blood sugar should usually be checked as small or high.

The 42-hour fast

It is adding six hours to the 36 hours fast, resulting in a fast of forty-two hours carried out about two times a week.

The 5:2 fast

This technique is conducted to prevent you from totally abstaining from meals and having cycles of calorie consumption. These calories are reduced to a rate that leads to many hormonal advantages of fasting. Five days of regular feeding with two days of fasting. With some protein and oil-based sauce or green vegetables and half an avocado, you can eat some vegetable salad during these fasting days; furthermore, do not eat any dinner. These days of fasting can be placed randomly or following each other in a week at specific times. This method is designed to create faster for more people, as many find it challenging to avoid eating altogether. There's no exact time to follow; as soon as you want, you can follow it.

The alternate-day fast

It may seem similar to the 5:2 fasting regimen, but it is not. It's fasting every day. This technique can be followed until you lose as much weight as you want, then you can reduce days of fasting. It allows weight loss to be maintained.

It is possible to move to different fasting regimens as your schedule can change. Intermittent fasting is not about a time-limiting eating window; it is flexible, so you can move your eating and fasting time to suit you, but don't keep changing them all the time; this reduces the effect of fasting on your body. You can even combine some fasting regiments like the 5:2 technique and the 24-hour fasting by having lunch before your fasting day at a particular moment and adding only lunch at the fasting lunch and doing the same for the following fasting day. With this, for twenty-four hours, you could not eat any calories and set your days of fasting as in the 5:2 method of fasting. Choose the fasting day technique that works well with you and can synchronize with your life.

A schedule allows you to create a routine after frequent fasting that makes it easier to integrate into your life. You can plan, but there's no problem if you can't. Even if you can't plan to fast, you should be open-minded to fasting to opportunities. You can fast every month or every year. Frankly, you won't lose weight on losing annual fasts.

Pros

1. When you are deciding which form of fasting is best for you, it is beneficial to keep in mind that intermittent fasting can be safer than water fasting for longer periods of time (as many people do) as it involves much shorter durations of fasting, making it better for those who are not as comfortable fasting for longer periods.
2. For women, there are some benefits to fasting that are different than those for men. Most notably, are the benefits that it has on the heart for women. Things like blood pressure and cholesterol can lead to severe and life-threatening heart diseases, and fasting has been shown to improve heart health in women.
3. It also improves the efficiency with which the bodies of women use insulin to control blood sugar.

Cons

1. There is some evidence that suggests that Intermittent Fasting affects men and women differently. Some studies have shown that in men, Intermittent Fasting helped their bodies to more efficiently regulate blood Sugar, while in women, this was not the case, and the regulation of blood sugar actually worsened. Another notable difference is that
2. Fasting, in general, may be harmful to some populations such as the elderly, women trying to conceive, and people with a history of eating disorders
3. There are some populations who should not fast due to the health risks it may pose. While fasting can provide health benefits, the following groups of people should not do so without first consulting a medical professional.

   - **Those Who Have Kidney Problems**

     People suffering from kidney disease need more calories than people who are in good health. They need the Nutrition that these calories provide them with as well. For this reason, those with kidney problems such as kidney stones, kidney failure, or any other disease of the kidneys should not participate in fasting.

   - **Those Who Have Liver Problems**

     Fasting is hard on the liver, as it is the liver that makes the ketones that the body uses for energy during fasting when carbohydrates are not available. If the liver is already stressed by disease, it is not a good idea to put further stress on the liver by then fasting.

   - **Women Who Are Trying to Conceive**

     When women are trying to conceive, their bodies are sensitive to the state of the internal environment of the body. This is because the body will not allow conception if the environment is not ideal for the growth of a healthy fetus. It is important to ensure that your body is in good shape and has enough nutrients if you are trying to conceive so that the body is confident in the fact that it will be able to grow a healthy baby.

   - **Those Who Are Underweight**

     If you are underweight, your body will not have access to the fat stores that it would turn to in the event of a fast. In this case, fasting can be dangerous because without these fat stores to break down for energy, the body can then reach a state of severe lack of energy and nutrients

- **Those Who Are Pregnant**

  When pregnant, your body is attempting to grow a healthy baby. In order to do this, the baby cannot go without the proper nutrients and food that it needs to grow, everything that you ingest while pregnant will be shared with your baby through the umbilical cord. If you do not have enough nutrients, the development of the baby could suffer.

- **Those Who Are Breastfeeding**

  While breastfeeding, the nutrients and minerals from everything that the mother ingests are passed to the baby through the milk. There are studies that show that the taste of breast milk can change depending on what the mother has most recently ingested. For this reason, it is important that the mother remains nourished and fed so that the baby is getting proper nourishment as well. The first few months, while the mother is breastfeeding, are essential to the development of the baby and breast milk is the main reason for this. Keeping breast milk full of nutrients is essential.

- **Women Who Have Irregular Periods**

  It has been shown that fasting can cause women to have irregular periods due to the changes in hormone production and secretion that it can cause. Those who experience this already should avoid fasting without consulting a doctor first.

- **Those with a History of Eating Disorders**

  For people who have a history of eating disorders of any sort, diets can be quite tricky. It is important for these people to be careful when restricting or controlling food intake in any way. Food-related planning and restricting can act as a trigger for those who have a history of eating disorders. It is not recommended that those people participate in intermittent fasting or fasting of any sort.

- **The Elderly**

  The elderly is at a vulnerable age as they are more susceptible to diseases and illnesses of any sort. They also tend to be smaller in size and have less body fat than they did when they were younger. For these reasons, it is not advised that they use fasting as a form of health improvement. This population needs all of the nutrients that they receive from the foods they eat, as well as the regular blood sugar levels that come with ingesting food regularly throughout the day. As they do not have as much fat stored in their bodies, they will not have the fat to break down for energy while fasting. Because of this, fasting can be dangerous for the elderly.

- **Those Who Are Below the Age of Eighteen**

  For people who are in their teen years, or especially children, fasting is not a necessary tool for weight loss or health improvement. Any sort of diet that involves fasting is not advisable for this population as they are still growing and developing and are in need of all of the nutrients that they ingest. They also tend to be more active, and because of this, they likely use up more than the number of calories that they eat on a daily basis. At these ages, the body is in need of calories to allow it to grow and change in the proper ways to prepare it for adulthood.

- **Those Who Have Conditions of the Heart**

  Those with conditions of the heart should take extra care if they are fasting for religious reasons, and otherwise should avoid fasting altogether. This is because their medication schedule is very rigid, and it must be taken with food. As this is not a medication schedule that can be adjusted, fasting is not a good idea for patients with this type of medication schedule. Further, some heart patients experience shortness of breath, or lightheadedness and fasting can exacerbate these symptoms if blood sugar becomes low. As there are many different types of heart conditions, it is necessary to consult a physician before deciding if fasting is right for you.

- **Those with Diabetes**

  As those with diabetes have struggled with their blood Sugar, fasting is likely not a good choice for them. When you fast, your body must find other sources of sugar in order to maintain blood sugar, and in people with diabetes, this can cause complications for their already sensitive blood sugar levels. For people with diabetes, having their blood sugar reach levels that are too high or too low can be very dangerous as their body has a hard time regulating this. Fasting may pose serious health risks for this population.

Side-Effects Associated with Intermittent Fasting

Another factor that could be considered a con when it comes to Intermittent Fasting is that there may be some side effects that accompany it. This is highly dependent on your body and the type of fasting that you choose to do, but it is definitely worth noting that some of the following side-effects may come about.

When it comes to side effects, the number one side-effect of fasting is hunger, as I'm sure you can imagine. You may also experience light-headedness and weakness, especially if you are just beginning to add fasting into your diet regime.

There are some side-effects that are to be expected when beginning a fast. These are not necessarily a cause for concern, as they are signs of your body adapting to a fast.

Regular side-effects of fasting include:

- Hunger
- Slight dehydration
- Headache
- Irritability
- Lower energy levels
- Constipation
- Lower body temperature

Getting Started

Intermittent fasting works best when it is paired with a healthy Dietary approach. The ketogenic diet, in this regard, rightly complements the intermittent fasting as it provides a good amount of lasting energy to the dieter during the fast. carbs are the immediate source of energy that is quickly metabolized and used, whereas fats provide energy through a gradual breakdown, which keeps the dieter energized during the fast. Thus, experts recommend a high fat and a low-carb diet to harness the true benefits of intermittent fasting.

1. **Follow the Caloric Limit**

Every method of intermittent fasting prescribes a certain caloric limit, which must be taken into consideration while planning a ketogenic meal for a fasting day. Reduce the number of calories without compromising on the balanced proportion of both the micro and macronutrients. Take more smoothies and zero caloric juices to keep the caloric intake in check. During the non-fasting days of the week, the meal plan must be followed through with a balanced approach, which must include small and frequent meals throughout the day.

2. **Depend More on fats**

The meal before the fast holds more important! It should be rich in fats so that the body will receive a constant supply of energy throughout the day. Use different sources of fats in one meal to keep a variety of flavors.

3. **Slowly Break the Fast**

Eating everything at once at the time of breaking the fast is going to reverse the effects of fasting. Even when you are on a ketogenic diet, you must break the fast with a small meal like a smoothie, then take a break and have another small meal. In this way, the excess fats will not be stored in the body.

4. **Focus on Hydration**

Intermittent fasting does not restrict a person from having zero caloric fluids and water. Since the ketogenic lifestyle demands more hydration, a person must constantly consume water during the fast and after it to keep the body hydrated all the time. Muscle and body Fatigue can be avoided with active hydration.

5. **Make Smart Choices**

Since fasting reduces the overall meal consumption during a day or a week, it requires better and healthy food to meet the nutritional needs of the body. A person does not need fillers on this diet; he must consume rich food with a variety of protein sources like meat and seafood along with nuts, oils, and vegetables. Make smarter choices and try to add multiple low-carb Ingredients in a single platter to have all the essential nutrients in every meal.

Super Foods

For women over 50, it seems that most food we eat doesn't go where we want it to! Fortunately, there are foods that can help accelerate the fat loss that will help you avoid feeling hungry and tired all of the time. So, what is a fat-burning food exactly?

In order for a food to be considered fat burning, it needs to be characterized by the following:

- Promotes Ketosis
- Increases Energy Levels without Many calories
- Improves Gut Health
- Reduces Calorie Consumption
- Increases Calorie Burning
- Are Highly Satiating

Below, you will find a list of fat-loss foods that will help jump-start your new diet. While other foods are going to be important for your overall health, try to incorporate the following to help out your results on the Ketogenic Diet.

Avocados

Avocados are so famous nowadays in the health community that people associate the word "health" with avocados. This is for a very good reason because avocados are very healthy. They pack lots of vitamins and minerals such as potassium. Moreover, avocados are shown to help the body go into ketosis faster.

Berries

Many fruits pack too many carbs that make them unsuitable in a keto diet, but not berries. They are low in carbs and high in Fiber. Some of the best berries to include in your diet are blackberries, blueberries, raspberries, and strawberries.

Butter and Cream

These two food items pack plenty of fat and a very small amount of carbs, making them a good option to include in your keto diet.

Cheese

Milk is not okay. You can get away with cheese though. Cheese is delicious and nutritious. Thankfully, although there are hundreds of types of cheese out there, all of them are low in carbs and full of fat. Eating cheese may even help your muscles and slow down aging.

Coconut Oil

Coconut oil and other coconut-related products such as coconut milk and coconut powder are perfect for a keto diet. Coconut oil, especially, contain MCTs that are converted into ketones by the liver to be used as an immediate source of energy.

Dark Chocolate and Cocoa Powder

These two food items are delicious and contain antioxidants. Dark chocolate is associated with the reduction of heart disease risk by lowering the blood pressure. Just make sure that you choose only dark chocolate with at least 70% cocoa solids.

Eggs

Eggs form the bulk of most food you will eat in a keto diet because they are the healthiest and most versatile food item of them all. Even a large egg contains so little carbs but packs plenty of protein, making it a perfect option for a keto diet.

Moreover, eggs are shown to have an appetite suppression effect, making you feel full for longer as well as regulating blood sugar levels. This leads to a lower calorie intake for about a day. Just make sure to eat the entire egg because the nutrients are in the yolk.

Meat and Poultry

These two are the staple food in most keto diets. Most of the keto meals revolve around using these two Ingredients. This is because they contain no carbs and pack plenty of vitamins and minerals. Moreover, they are a great source of protein.

Nuts and Seeds

These are also low in carbs but rich in fat. They are also healthy and have a lot of nutrients and Fiber. They help reduce heart disease, cancer, depression, and other risks of diseases. The Fiber in these also help make you feel full for longer, so you would consume fewer calories and your body would spend more calories digesting them.

Olive Oil

Olive oil is very beneficial for your heart because it contains oleic acid that helps decrease heart disease risk factors. Extra-virgin olive oil is also rich in antioxidants. The best thing is that olive oil can be used as a main source of fat and it has no carbs. The same goes for olive.

Plain Greek Yogurt and Cottage Cheese

These two food items are rich in protein and a small number of carbs, small enough that you can safely include them in your keto diet. They also help suppress your appetite by making you feel full for longer and they can be eaten alone and are still delicious.

Seafood

Fishes and shellfishes are perfect for keto diets. Many fishes are rich in B vitamins, potassium, as well as selenium. Salmon, sardines, mackerel, and other Fatty fish also pack a lot of omega-3 fats that help in regulating insulin levels. These are so low in carbs that it is negligible.

Shellfishes are a different story because some contain very few carbs whereas others pack plenty. Shrimps and most crabs are okay but beware of other types of shellfish.

Shirataki Noodles

If you love noodles and pasta but don't want to give up on them, then shirataki noodles are the perfect alternative. They are rich in water content and pack a lot of Fiber, so that means low carbs and calories and hunger suppression.

Unsweetened Coffee and Tea

These two drinks are carb-free, so long as you don't add sugar, milk, or any other sweeteners. Both contain caffeine that improves your metabolism and suppresses your appetite. A word of warning to those who love light coffee and tea lattes, though. They are made with non-Fat milk and contain a lot of carbs.

Vegetables

As you start the Ketogenic Diet, you may find that finding low-carb vegetables is going to be a difficult task. One of the approved vegetable groups would include cruciferous vegetables such as cauliflower and broccoli. These foods provide an excellent source of Fiber and sulforaphane. Sulforaphane is a compound that activates cell-protecting pathways to help protect your cells from oxidative stress. When this process occurs, it helps remove toxins from your body. When you are less stressed, it helps you become less fat.

CHAPTER 9:

30 Day-Meal Plan

Day	Breakfast	Lunch	Dinner	Snacks/Dessert
1	Mediterranean Breakfast Egg White Sandwich	Pork and Bean Stew	Tasty Lamb Leg	Yogurt Dip
2	Greek Yogurt with Walnuts and Honey	Mediterranean Lamb Chops	Balearic Beef Brisket Bowl	Pepper Tapenade
3	Feta-Avocado & Mashed Chickpea Toast	Pork and Greens Salad	Lamb Burger	Wrapped Plums
4	Smoked Salmon and Poached Eggs on Toast	Perfect Chicken & Rice	Chicken Marsala	Smoked Salmon Crudités
5	Mediterranean Feta and Quinoa Egg Muffins	Easy Honey-Garlic Pork Chops	Orange and Garlic Shrimp	Pecan and Carrot Cake
6	Strawberry and Rhubarb Smoothie	Turkey Meatballs	Salmon Baked in Foil	Coriander Falafel
7	Bacon and Brie Omelet Wedges	Slow Cooker Salmon in Foil	Kale Sprouts & Lamb	Simple Apple Compote
8	Pearl Couscous Salad	Balsamic-Honey Glazed Salmon	Pork With Couscous	Spiced Sweet Pecans
9	Crumbled Feta and Scallions	Pork Strips and Rice	Lemon Garlic Shrimp	Mini Nuts and Fruits Crumble
10	Date and Walnut Overnight Oats	Greek Meatballs	Artichoke Olive Chicken	Mint Banana Chocolate Sorbet
11	Cauliflower Fritters with Hummus	Chicken Shish Tawook	Mediterranean Beef Skewers	Olive Tapenade With Anchovies
12	Blueberry Greek Yogurt Pancakes	Mushroom and Beef Risotto	Easy Chicken Scampi	Red Pepper Hummus
13	Overnight Berry Chia Oats	Greek Pork	Greek Chicken Rice	Stuffed Avocado

14	Quinoa Bake With Banana	Dill Chutney Salmon	Flank Steak With Artichokes	Tuna Croquettes
15	Artichoke Frittata	Moussaka	Yogurt-Marinated Chicken	Eggplant Dip
16	Tomato and Dill Frittata	Creamy Chicken Breasts	Tuna and Zucchini Patties	Bulgur Lamb Meatballs
17	Cheesy Olives Bread	Flavorful Chicken Tacos	Sesame Beef	Peanut Butter and Chocolate Balls
18	Stuffed Pita Breads	Mediterranean Lamb Bowl	Sole Piccata With Capers	Veggie Fritters
19	Blueberries Quinoa	Chicken Skewers With Veggies	Worcestershire Pork Chops	White Bean Dip
20	Gnocchi Ham Olives	Beef & Potatoes	Greek Lemon Chicken Kebabs	Apple and Berries Ambrosia
21	Pastry-Less Spanakopita	Pesto Vegetable Chicken	Rosemary Pork Chops	Glazed Pears With Hazelnuts
22	Feta Frittata	Easy Chicken Piccata	Seafood Risotto	Berry and Rhubarb Cobbler
23	Mediterranean Eggs	Baked Fish With Pistachio Crust	Roasted Pork With Apple-Dijon Sauce	Chocolate and Avocado Mousse
24	Full Eggs in a Squash	Quick Herbed Lamb and Pasta	Feta Stuffed Chicken Breasts	Cucumber Sandwich Bites
25	Pear and Mango Smoothie	Chicken From Milan	Pressure Cooker Moroccan Pot Roast	Coconut Blueberries With Brown Rice
26	Sweet Potato Tart	Tender Lamb	Grilled Lemon Pesto Salmon	Tomato Bruschetta
27	Spicy Early Morning Seafood Risotto	Crispy Herb Crusted Halibut	Cumin Lamb Mix	Marinated Feta and Artichokes
28	Coconut Porridge	Tender Chicken & Mushrooms	Pepper Tilapia With Spinach	Lemon Crockpot Cake
29	Barley Porridge	Beef and Chili Mix	Pistachio Sole Fish	Raspberry Yogurt Basted Cantaloupe
30	Eggplant Salad	Moroccan Chicken	Hazelnut Crusted Sea Bass	Cucumber Bites

CHAPTER 10:

Breakfast

1. Greek Yogurt with Fresh Berries, Honey, and Nuts

Preparation Time: 5 minutes.
Cooking Time: 0 minutes.
Servings: 1
Ingredients:

- 6 oz. non-fat plain Greek yogurt.
- ½ cup fresh berries of your choice.
- 1 tbsp. 25 oz. crushed walnuts.
- 1 tbsp. honey.

Directions:
1. In a jar with a lid, add the yogurt. Top with berries and a drizzle of honey. Top with the lid and store in the fridge for 2 to 3 days.

Nutrition:

- Calories: 250.
- Protein: 19 g.
- Fat: 4 g.
- Carbs: 35 g.

2. Quinoa Bake With Banana

Preparation Time: 15 minutes.
Cooking Time: 1 hour & 10 minutes.
Servings: 8
Ingredients:

- 3 cups medium over-ripe bananas, mashed.
- ¼ cup molasses.
- ¼ cup pure maple syrup.
- 1 tbsp. cinnamon.
- 2 tsp. raw vanilla extract.
- 1 tsp. ground ginger.
- 1 tsp. ground cloves.
- ½ tsp. ground allspice.
- ½ tsp. salt.
- 1 cup quinoa, uncooked.
- 2 ½ cups unsweetened vanilla almond milk.
- ¼ cup slivered almonds

Directions:
1. In the bottom of a 2-1/2-3-quart casserole dish, mix together the mashed banana, maple syrup, cinnamon, vanilla extract, ginger, cloves, allspice, molasses, and salt until well mixed.
2. Add in the quinoa; stir until the quinoa is evenly in the banana mixture. Whisk in the almond milk, mix until well combined, cover, and refrigerate overnight or bake immediately.
3. Heat oven to 350°F. Whisk the quinoa mixture making sure it doesn't settle to the bottom.
4. Cover the pan with tinfoil and bake until the liquid is absorbed, and the top of the quinoa is set, for about 1 hour to 1 hour and 15 minutes.
5. Turn the oven to high broil, uncover the pan, sprinkle with sliced almonds, and lightly press them into the quinoa.
6. Broil until the almonds just turn golden brown, about 2 to 4 minutes, watching closely, as they burn quickly. Allow to cool for 10 minutes then slice the quinoa bake
7. Distribute the quinoa bake among the containers, store in the fridge for 3 to 4 days.

Nutrition:

- Calories: 213.
- Protein: 5 g.
- Fat: 4 g.
- Carbs: 41 g.

3. Italian Breakfast Sausage with Baby Potatoes and Vegetables

Preparation Time: 15 minutes.
Cooking Time: 30 minutes.
Servings: 4
Ingredients:

- 1 pound sweet Italian sausage links, sliced on the bias (diagonal).
- 2 cups baby potatoes, halved.
- 2 cups broccoli florets.
- 1 cup onions cut into 1-inch chunks.
- 2 cups small mushrooms -half or quarter the large ones for uniform size.
- 1 cup baby carrots.
- 2 tbsp. olive oil.

- ½ tsp. garlic powder.
- ½ tsp. Italian seasoning.
- 1 tsp. salt.
- ½ tsp. pepper.

Directions:

1. Preheat the oven to 400°F. In a large bowl, add the baby potatoes, broccoli florets, onions, small mushrooms, and baby carrots.
2. Add in the olive oil, salt, pepper, garlic powder, and Italian seasoning and toss to evenly coat. Spread the vegetables onto a sheet pan in one even layer.
3. Arrange the sausage slices on the pan over the vegetables. Bake for 30 minutes. Make sure to sake halfway through to prevent sticking. Allow cooling.
4. Distribute the Italian sausages and vegetables among the containers and store them in the fridge for 2 to 3 days

Nutrition:

- Calories: 321.
- Protein: 22 g.
- Fat: 16 g.
- Carbs: 23 g.

4. Sun-Dried Tomatoes, Dill and Feta Omelet Casserole

Preparation Time: 15 minutes.
Cooking Time: 40 minutes.
Servings: 6
Ingredients:

- 12 large eggs.
- 2 cups whole milk.
- 8 oz. fresh spinach.
- 2 garlic cloves, minced.
- 12 oz. artichoke salad with olives and peppers, drained and chopped.
- 5 oz. sun-dried tomato feta cheese, crumbled.
- 1 tbsp. fresh chopped dill or 1 tsp. dried dill
- 1 tsp. dried oregano.
- 1 tsp. lemon pepper.
- 1 tsp. salt.
- 4 tsp. olive oil, divided.

Directions:

1. Preheat oven to 375°F. Chop the fresh herbs and artichoke salad. In a skillet over medium heat, add 1 tbsp. olive oil.
2. Sauté the spinach and garlic until wilted, about 3 minutes. Oil a 9x13 inch baking dish, layer the spinach and artichoke salad evenly in the dish

3. In a medium bowl, whisk together the eggs, milk, herbs, salt, and lemon pepper. Pour the egg mixture over vegetables, sprinkle with feta cheese.
4. Bake in the center of the oven for 35 to 40 minutes until firm in the center. Allow to cool, slice, and distribute among the storage containers. Store for 2 to 3 days or freeze for 3 months

Nutrition:

- Calories: 196.
- Protein: 10 g.
- Fat: 12 g.
- Carbs: 5 g.

5. Mediterranean Breakfast Egg White Sandwich

Preparation Time: 15 minutes.
Cooking Time: 30 minutes.
Servings: 1
Ingredients:

- 1 tsp. vegan butter.
- ¼ cup egg whites.
- 1 tsp. chopped fresh herbs such as parsley, basil, rosemary.
- 1 whole-grain seeded ciabatta roll.
- 1 tbsp. pesto.
- 1 or 2 slices Muenster cheese (or other cheese such as provolone, Monterey Jack, etc.)
- About ½ cup roasted tomatoes.
- Salt, to taste.
- Pepper, to taste.

For Roasted tomatoes:

- 10 oz. grape tomatoes.
- 1 tbsp. extra virgin olive oil.
- Kosher salt, to taste.
- Coarse black pepper, to taste.

Directions:

1. In a small nonstick skillet over medium heat, melt the vegan butter. Pour in egg whites, season with salt and pepper, sprinkle with fresh herbs, cook for 3 to 4 minutes or until egg is done, flip once.
2. In the meantime, toast the ciabatta bread in the toaster. Once done, spread both halves with pesto.
3. Place the egg on the bottom half of sandwich rolls, folding if necessary, top with cheese, add the roasted tomatoes, and top half of roll sandwich.
4. For the roasted tomatoes, preheat the oven to 400°F. Slice tomatoes in half lengthwise. Then place them onto a baking sheet and drizzle with the olive oil, toss to coat.
5. Season with salt and pepper and roast in the oven for about 20 minutes, until the skin appears wrinkled

Nutrition:
- Calories: 458.
- Protein: 21 g.
- Fat: 0 g.
- Carbs: 51 g.

6. Breakfast Taco Scramble

Preparation Time: 15 minutes.
Cooking Time: 1 hour & 25 minutes.
Servings: 4
Ingredients:
- 8 large eggs, beaten.
- ¼ tsp. seasoning salt.
- 1 pound 99% lean ground turkey.
- 2 tbsp. Greek seasoning.
- ½ small onion, minced.
- 2 tbsp. bell pepper, minced.
- 4 oz. can tomato sauce.
- ¼ cup water.
- ¼ cup chopped scallions or cilantro, for topping.

For the potatoes:
- 12 (1 pound) Baby gold or red potatoes, quartered.
- 4 tsp. olive oil.
- ¾ tsp. salt.
- ½ tsp. garlic powder.
- Fresh black pepper, to taste.

Directions:
1. In a large bowl, beat the eggs, season with seasoning salt. Preheat the oven to 425°F.

Spray a 9x12 or large oval casserole dish with cooking oil.

2. Add the potatoes 1 tbsp. oil, ¾ tsp. salt, garlic powder, and black pepper and toss to coat. Bake for 45 minutes to 1 hour, tossing every 15 minutes.
3. In the meantime, brown the turkey in a large skillet over medium heat, breaking it up while it cooks. Once no longer pink, add in the Greek seasoning.
4. Add in the bell pepper, onion, tomato sauce, and water, stir and cover, simmer on low for about 20 minutes. Spray a different skillet with nonstick spray over medium heat.
5. Once heated, add in the eggs seasoned with ¼ tsp. of salt and scramble for 2 to 3 minutes, or cook until it sets.
6. Distribute ¾ cup turkey and ²/₃ cup eggs and divide the potatoes in each storage container, store for 3 to 4 days.

Nutrition:
- Calories: 450.
- Protein: 46 g.
- Fat: 19 g.
- Carbs: 24.5 g.

7. Blueberry Greek Yogurt Pancakes

Preparation Time: 15 minutes.
Cooking Time: 15 minutes.
Servings: 6
Ingredients:
- 1 ¼ cup all-purpose flour.
- 2 tsp. baking powder.
- 1 tsp. baking soda.
- ¼ tsp. salt.
- ¼ cup Sugar.
- 3 eggs.
- 3 tbsp. vegan butter unsalted, melted.

- ½ cup milk.
- 1 ½ cups Greek yogurt plain, non-Fat.
- ½ cup blueberries, optional.

Toppings:

- Greek yogurt.
- Mixed berries (blueberries, raspberries, and blackberries.)

Directions:

1. In a large bowl, whisk together the flour, salt, baking powder, and baking soda. In a separate bowl, whisk together butter, sugar, eggs, Greek yogurt, and milk until the mixture is smooth.
2. Then add in the Greek yogurt mixture from step to the dry mixture in step 1, mix to combine, allow the batter to sit for 20 minutes to get a smooth texture (if using blueberries fold them into the pancake batter.)
3. Heat the pancake griddle, spray with non-stick butter spray or just brush with butter. Pour the batter in ¼ cupful onto the griddle.
4. Cook until the bubbles on top burst and create small holes, lift up the corners of the pancake to see if they're golden brown on the bottom
5. With a wide spatula, flip the pancake and cook on the other side until lightly browned. Serve.

Nutrition:

- Calories: 258.
- Protein: 11g.
- Fat: 8 g.
- Carbs: 33 g.

8. Cauliflower Fritters with Hummus

Preparation Time: 15 minutes

Cooking Time: 15 minutes

Servings: 4

Ingredients:

- 2 (15 oz.) cans chickpeas, divided.
- 2 ½ tbsp. olive oil, divided, plus more for frying.
- 1 cup onion, chopped, about ½ a small onion.
- 2 tbsp. garlic, minced.
- 2 cups cauliflower, cut into small pieces, about ½ a large head.
- ½ tsp. salt.
- Black pepper.

Topping:

- Hummus, of choice.
- Green onion, diced.

Directions:

1. Preheat theoven to 400°F. Rinse and drain 1 can of the chickpeas, place them on a paper towel to dry off well.
2. Then place the chickpeas into a large bowl, removing the loose skins that come off, and toss with 1 tbsp. of olive oil, spread the chickpeas onto a large pan, and sprinkle with salt and pepper.
3. Bake for 20 minutes, then stir and then bake an additional 5 to 10 minutes until very crispy.
4. Once the chickpeas are roasted, transfer them to a large food processor and process them until broken down and crumble. Don't over-process them and turn them into flour, as you need to have some texture. Place the mixture into a small bowl, set aside.
5. In a large pan over medium-high heat, add the remaining 1 ½ tbsp. of olive oil. Once heated, add in the onion and garlic, cook until lightly golden brown, about 2 minutes.
6. Then add in the chopped cauliflower, cook for an additional 2 minutes, until the cauliflower is golden.
7. Turn the heat down to low and cover the pan, cook until the cauliflower is fork-tender and the onions are golden brown and caramelized, stirring often about 3 to 5 minutes.
8. Transfer the cauliflower mixture to the food processor, drain and rinse the remaining can of chickpeas and add them into the food processor, along with the salt and a pinch of pepper.
9. Blend until smooth, and the mixture starts to ball, stop to scrape down the sides as needed
10. Transfer the cauliflower mixture into a large bowl and add in ½ cup of the roasted chickpea crumbs, stir until well combined.
11. In a large bowl over medium heat, add in enough oil to lightly cover the bottom of a large pan. Working in batches, cook the patties until golden brown, about 2 to 3 minutes, flip and cook again. Serve.

Nutrition:

- Calories: 333.
- Protein: 14 g.
- Fat: 13 g.
- Carbs: 45 g.

9. Overnight Berry Chia Oats

Preparation Time: 15 minutes.
Cooking Time: 5 minutes.
Servings: 1
Ingredients:

- ½ cup Quaker oats rolled oats.
- ¼ cup chia seeds.
- 1 cup milk or water.
- Pinch salt and cinnamon.
- Maple syrup, or a different sweetener, to taste.
- 1 cup frozen berries of choice or smoothie leftovers.

Toppings:

- Yogurt.
- Berries.

Directions:

1. In a jar with a lid, add the oats, seeds, milk, salt, and cinnamon, refrigerate overnight. On serving day, puree the berries in a blender.
2. Stir the oats, add in the berry puree, and top with yogurt and more berries, nuts, honey, or garnish of your choice. Enjoy!

Nutrition:

- Calories: 405.
- Protein: 17 g.
- Fat: 11 g.
- Carbs: 65 g.

10. 5-Minute Heirloom Tomato & Cucumber Toast

Preparation Time: 10 minutes.
Cooking Time: 6 to 10 minutes.
Servings: 1
Ingredients:

- 1 small Heirloom tomato.
- 1 Persian cucumber.
- 1 tsp. olive oil.
- 1 pinch oregano.

- Kosher salt and pepper as desired.
- 2 tsp. low-Fat whipped cream cheese.
- 2 pieces Trader Joe's whole grain crispbread or your choice.
- 1 tsp. Balsamic glaze.

Directions:

1. Dice the cucumber and tomato. Combine all the fixings except for the cream cheese. Smear the cheese on the bread and add the mixture. Top it off with the balsamic glaze and serve.

Nutrition:

- Calories: 239.
- Protein: 7 g.
- Fat: 11 g.
- Carbs: 32 g.

11. Greek Yogurt with Walnuts and Honey

Preparation Time: 5 minutes.
Cooking Time: 0 minutes.
Servings: 4
Ingredients:

- 4 cups Greek yogurt, Fat-free, plain, or vanilla.
- ½ cup California walnuts, toasted, chopped.
- 3 tbsp. honey or agave nectar.
- Fresh fruit, chopped or granola, low-Fat (both optional).

Directions:

1. Spoon yogurt into 4 individual cups. Sprinkle 2 tbsp. of walnuts over each and drizzle 2 tsp. of honey over each. Top with fruit or granola, whichever is preferred.

Nutrition:

- Calories: 300.
- Protein: 29 g.
- Fat: 10 g.
- Carbs: 25 g.

12. Tahini Pine Nuts Toast

Preparation Time: 5 minutes.
Cooking Time: 0 minutes.
Servings: 2
Ingredients:

- 2 whole-wheat bread slices, toasted.
- 1 tsp. water
- 1 tbsp. tahini paste.
- 2 tsp. feta cheese, crumbled.
- ½ lemon, juiced.
- 2 tsp. pine nuts.
- A pinch black pepper.

Directions:
1. In a bowl, mix the tahini with the water and the lemon juice, whisk well, and spread over the toasted bread slices.
2. Top each serving with the remaining Ingredients and serve for breakfast.

Nutrition:
- Calories: 142. Protein: 5.8 g.
- Fat: 7.6 g. Carbs: 13.7 g.

13. Feta-Avocado & Mashed Chickpea Toast

Preparation Time: 10 minutes.
Cooking Time: 15 minutes.
Servings: 4
Ingredients:
- 15 oz. can chickpeas.
- 2 oz. or ½ cup diced feta cheese.
- 1 pitted avocado.

For fresh juice:
- 2 tsp. lemon (or 1 tbsp. orange)
- ½ tsp. black pepper. - 2 tsp. honey.
- 4 slices multigrain toast.

Directions:
1. Toast the bread. Drain the chickpeas in a colander. Scoop the avocado flesh into the bowl. Use a large fork/potato masher to mash them until the mix is spreadable.
2. Pour in the lemon juice, pepper, and feta. Combine and divide onto the 4 slices of toast. Drizzle using the honey and serve.

Nutrition:
- Calories: 337. Protein: 13 g.
- Fat: 13 g. Carbs: 43 g.

14. Feta Frittata

Preparation Time: 15 minutes.
Cooking Time: 25 minutes.
Servings: 2
Ingredients:
- 1 small garlic clove.
- 1 green onion.
- 2 large eggs.
- ½ cup egg substitute.
- 4 tbsp. crumbled feta cheese, divided.
- $\frac{1}{3}$ Cup plum tomato.
- 4 thin avocado slices.
- 2 tbsp. reduced-Fat sour cream.
- Also needed: 6-inch skillet.

Directions:
1. Thinly slice/mince the onion, garlic, and tomato. Peel the avocado before slicing. Heat the pan using the medium temperature setting and spritz it with cooking oil.
2. Whisk the egg substitute, eggs, and feta cheese. Add the egg mixture into the pan. Cover and simmer for four to six minutes.
3. Sprinkle it using the rest of the feta cheese and tomato. Cover and continue cooking until the eggs are set or about 2 to 3 more minutes.
4. Wait for about 5 minutes before cutting it into halves. Serve with avocado and sour cream.

Nutrition:
- Calories: 460.
- Protein: 24 g.
- Fat: 37 g.
- Carbs: 8 g.

15. Smoked Salmon and Poached Eggs on Toast

Preparation Time: 10 minutes.
Cooking Time: 4 minutes.
Servings: 4
Ingredients:
- 2 oz. avocado smashed.
- 2 slices bread toasted.
- Pinch kosher salt and cracked black pepper.
- ¼ tsp. freshly squeezed lemon juice.
- 2 eggs see notes, poached.
- 3.5 oz. smoked salmon.
- 1 tbsp. thinly sliced scallions.
- Splash Kikkoman soy sauce, optional.
- Microgreens are optional.

Directions:
1. Take a small bowl and then smash the avocado into it. Then, add the lemon juice and also a pinch of salt into the mixture. Then, mix it well and set it aside.
2. After that, poach the eggs and toast the bread for some time. Once the bread is toasted, you will have to spread the avocado on both slices

and after that, add the smoked salmon to each slice.

3. Thereafter, carefully transfer the poached eggs to the respective toasts. Add a splash of Kikkoman soy sauce and some cracked pepper; then, just garnish with scallions and microgreens.

Nutrition:

- Calories: 459.
- Protein: 31 g.
- Fat: 22 g.
- Carbs: 33 g.

16. Low-Carb Baked Eggs with Avocado and Feta

Preparation Time: 10 minutes.
Cooking Time: 15 minutes.
Servings: 2
Ingredients:

- 1 avocado.
- 4 eggs.
- 2 to 3 tbsp. crumbled feta cheese.
- Nonstick cooking spray.
- Pepper and salt to taste.

Directions:

1. First, you will have to preheat the oven to 400°F. After that, when the oven is at the proper temperature, you will have to put the gratin dishes right on the baking sheet.
2. Then, leave the dishes to heat in the oven for almost 10 minutes. After that process, you need to break the eggs into individual ramekins.
3. Then, let the avocado and eggs come to room temperature for at least 10 minutes. Then, peel the avocado properly and cut it each half into 6 to 8 slices.
4. You will have to remove the dishes from the oven and spray them with non-stick spray. Then, you will have to arrange all the sliced avocados in the dishes and tip 2 eggs into each dish. Sprinkle with feta, add pepper and salt to taste, serve.

Nutrition:

- Calories: 280.
- Protein: 11 g.
- Fat: 23 g.
- Carbs: 10 g.

17. Mediterranean Eggs White Breakfast Sandwich with Roasted Tomatoes

Preparation Time: 15 minutes.
Cooking Time: 10 minutes.
Servings: 2
Ingredients:

- Salt and pepper to taste.
- ¼ cup egg whites.
- 1 tsp. chopped fresh herbs like rosemary, basil, and parsley.
- 1 whole-grain seeded ciabatta roll.
- 1 tsp. butter.
- 1 to 2 slices Muenster cheese.
- 1 tbsp. pesto.
- About ½ cup roasted tomatoes.
- 10 oz. grape tomatoes.
- 1 tbsp. extra-virgin olive oil.

Directions:

1. First, you will have to melt the butter over medium heat in the small nonstick skillet. Then, mix the egg whites with pepper and salt.
2. Then, sprinkle it with fresh herbs. After that cook it for almost 3 to 4 minutes or until the eggs are done, then flip it carefully.
3. Meanwhile, toast ciabatta bread in the toaster. Place the egg on the bottom half of the sandwich rolls, then top with cheese
4. Add roasted tomatoes and the top half of the roll. To make a roasted tomato, preheat the oven to 400°F. Then, slice the tomatoes in half lengthwise.
5. Place on the baking sheet and drizzle with olive oil. Season it with pepper and salt and then roast in the oven for about 20 minutes. Skins will appear wrinkled when done.

Nutrition:

- Calories: 458.
- Protein: 21 g.
- Fat: 24 g.
- Carbs: 51 g.

18. Greek Yogurt Pancakes

Preparation Time: 10 minutes.
Cooking Time: 5 minutes.
Servings: 2
Ingredients:

- 1 cup all-purpose flour.
- 1 cup whole-wheat flour.

- ¼ tsp. salt.
- 4 tsp. baking powder.
- 1 tbsp. Sugar.
- 1 ½ cups unsweetened almond milk.
- 2 tsp. vanilla extract.
- 2 large eggs.
- ½ cup plain 2% Greek yogurt.
- Fruit, for serving.
- Maple syrup, for serving.

Directions:

1. First, you will have to pour the curds into the bowl and mix them well until creamy. After that, you will have to add egg whites and mix them well until combined.
2. Then take a separate bowl, pour the wet mixture into the dry mixture. Stir to combine. The batter will be extremely thick.
3. Then, simply spoon the batter onto the sprayed pan heated too medium-high. The batter must make 4 large pancakes.
4. Then, you will have to flip the pancakes once when they start to bubble a bit on the surface. Cook until golden brown on both sides.

Nutrition:

- Calories: 166.
- Protein: 14 g.
- Fat: 5 g.
- Carbs: 52 g.

19. Mediterranean Feta and Quinoa Egg Muffins

Preparation Time: 15 minutes.

Cooking Time: 15 minutes.

Servings: 12

Ingredients:

- 2 cups baby spinach finely chopped.
- 1 cup chopped or sliced cherry tomatoes.
- ½ cup finely chopped onion.
- 1 tbsp. chopped fresh oregano.
- 1 cup crumbled feta cheese.
- ½ cup chopped {pitted} Kalamata olives.
- 2 tsp. high oleic sunflower oil.
- 1 cup cooked quinoa.
- 8 eggs.
- ¼ tsp. salt.

Directions:

1. Pre-heat oven to 350°F, and then prepare 12 silicone muffin holders on the baking sheet, or just grease a 12-cup muffin tin with oil and set aside.

2. Finely chop the vegetables and then heat the skillet to medium. After that, add the vegetable oil and onions and sauté for 2 minutes.
3. Then, add tomatoes and sauté for another minute then add spinach and sauté until wilted, about 1 minute.
4. Place the beaten egg into a bowl and then add lots of vegetables like feta cheese, quinoa, veggie mixture as well as salt, and then stir well until everything is properly combined.
5. Pour the ready mixture into greased muffin tins or silicone cups, dividing the mixture equally. Then, bake it in an oven for 30 minutes or so.

Nutrition:

- Calories: 113.
- Protein: 6 g.
- Fat: 7 g.
- Carbs: 5 g.

20. Mediterranean Eggs

Preparation Time: 15 minutes.

Cooking Time: 20 minutes.

Servings: 2

Ingredients:

- 5 tbsp. divided olive oil.
- 2 diced medium-sized Spanish onions.
- 2 diced red bell peppers.
- 2 minced garlic cloves.
- 1 tsp. cumin seeds.
- 4 diced large ripe tomatoes.
- 1 tbsp. honey.
- Salt.
- Freshly ground black pepper.
- $1/_3$ Cup crumbled feta.
- 4 eggs.
- 1 tsp. zaatar spice.
- Grilled pita during serving.

Directions:

1. Add 3 tbsp. of olive oil into a pan and heat it over medium heat. Along with the oil, sauté the cumin seeds, onions, garlic, and red pepper for a few minutes.
2. After that, add the diced tomatoes and salt and pepper to taste and cook them for about 10 minutes till they come together and form a light sauce.
3. With that, half the preparation is already done. Now you just have to break the eggs directly into the sauce and poach them.
4. However, you must keep in mind to cook the egg whites but keep the yolks still runny. This takes about 8 to 10 minutes.
5. While plating, add some feta and olive oil with za'atar spice to further enhance the flavors. Once done, serve with grilled pita.

Nutrition:

- Calories: 304.
- Protein: 12 g.
- Fat: 16 g.
- Carbs: 28 g.

21. Pastry-Less Spanakopita

Preparation Time: 5 minutes.
Cooking Time: 20 minutes.
Servings: 4
Ingredients:

- $1/8$ tsp. black pepper, add as per taste.
- $1/3$ cup extra virgin olive oil.
- 4 lightly beaten eggs.
- 7 cups lettuce, preferably a spring mix (mesclun).
- ½ cup crumbled feta cheese.
- $1/8$ tsp. sea salt, add to taste.
- 1 finely chopped medium yellow onion.

Directions:

1. Warm the oven to 180° C and grease the flan dish. Once done, pour the extra virgin olive oil into a large saucepan and heat it over medium heat with the onions, until they are translucent.
2. Add greens and keep stirring until all the Ingredients are wilted. Season it with salt and pepper and transfer the greens to the prepared dish and sprinkle on some feta cheese.
3. Pour the eggs and bake it for 20 minutes till it is cooked through and slightly brown.

Nutrition:

- Calories: 325.
- Protein: 11.2 g.
- Fat: 27.9 g.
- Carbs: 7.3 g.

22. Date and Walnut Overnight Oats

Preparation Time: 5 minutes.
Cooking Time: 20 minutes.
Servings: 2
Ingredients:

- ¼ cup Greek yogurt, plain.
- $1/3$ cup yogurt.
- $2/3$ cup oats.
- 1 cup milk.
- 2 tsp. date syrup or you can also use maple syrup or honey.
- 1 mashed banana.
- ¼ tsp. cinnamon.
- ¼ cup walnuts.
- Pinch salt (approx. $1/8$ tsp.)

Directions:

1. Firstly, get a mason jar or a small bowl and add all the Ingredients. After that stir and mix all the Ingredients well. Cover it securely, and cool it in a refrigerator overnight.
2. After that, take it out the next morning, add more liquid or cinnamon if required, and serve cold. (However, you can also microwave it for people with a warmer palate.)

Nutrition:

- Calories: 350.
- Protein: 14 g.
- Fat: 12 g.
- Carbs: 49 g.

23. Pear and Mango Smoothie

Preparation Time: 5 minutes.
Cooking Time: 0 minutes.
Servings: 1
Ingredients:

- 1 ripe mango, cored and chopped
- ½ mango, peeled, pitted, and chopped
- 1 cup kale, chopped
- ½ cup plain Greek yogurt
- 2 ice cubes

Directions:

1. Add pear, mango, yogurt, kale, and mango to a blender and puree.

2. Add ice and blend until you have a smooth texture. Serve and enjoy!

Nutrition:

- Calories: 293.
- Protein: 8 g.
- Fat: 8 g.
- Carbs: 53 g.

24. Eggplant Salad

Preparation Time: 20 minutes.
Cooking Time: 15 minutes.
Servings: 8
Ingredients:

- 1 large eggplant, washed and cubed.
- 1 tomato, seeded and chopped.
- 1 small onion, diced.
- 2 tbsp. parsley, chopped.
- 2 tbsp. extra virgin olive oil.
- 2 tbsp. distilled white vinegar.
- ½ cup feta cheese, crumbled.
- Salt as needed.

Directions:

1. Preheat your outdoor grill to medium-high. Pierce the eggplant a few times using a knife/fork. Cook the eggplants on your grill for about 15 minutes until they are charred.
2. Keep it on the side and allow them to cool. Remove the skin from the eggplant and dice the pulp. Transfer the pulp to a mixing bowl and add parsley, onion, tomato, olive oil, feta cheese, and vinegar.
3. Mix well and chill for 1 hour. Season with salt and enjoy!

Nutrition:

- Calories: 99.
- Protein: 3.4g.
- Fat: 7 g.
- Carbs: 7g.

25. Artichoke Frittata

Preparation Time: 5 minutes.
Cooking Time: 10 minutes.
Servings: 4
Ingredients:

- 8 large eggs.
- ¼ cup asiago cheese, grated.
- 1 tbsp. fresh basil, chopped.
- 1 tsp. fresh oregano, chopped.
- Pinch sea salt and pepper.
- 1 tsp. extra virgin olive oil.
- 1 tsp. garlic, minced.
- 1 cup canned artichokes, drained.
- 1 tomato, chopped.

Directions:

1. Pre-heat your oven to broil. Take a medium bowl and whisk in eggs, asiago cheese, oregano, basil, sea salt, and pepper. Blend in a bowl.
2. Place a large ovenproof skillet over medium-high heat and add olive oil. Add garlic and sauté for 1 minute. Remove the skillet from heat and pour in the egg mix.
3. Return skillet to heat and sprinkle artichoke hearts and tomato over eggs. Cook frittata without stirring for 8 minutes.
4. Place skillet under the broiler for 1 minute until the top is lightly browned. Cut frittata into 4 pieces and serve. Enjoy!

Nutrition:

- Calories: 199.
- Protein: 16 g.
- Fat: 13 g.
- Carbs: 5 g.

26. Full Eggs in a Squash

Preparation Time: 15 minutes.
Cooking Time: 20 minutes.
Servings: 5
Ingredients:

- 2 acorn squashes.
- 6 whole eggs.
- 2 tbsp. extra virgin olive oil.
- Salt and pepper as needed.
- 5 to 6 pitted dates.
- 8 walnut halves.
- Fresh bunch parsley.
- Maple syrup.

Directions:

1. Preheat your oven to 375°F. Slice squash crosswise and prepare 3 slices with holes. While slicing the squash, make sure that each slice has a measurement of ¾ inch thickness.
2. Remove the seeds from the slices. Take a baking sheet and line it with parchment paper. Transfer the slices to your baking sheet and season them with salt and pepper.
3. Bake in your oven for 20 minutes. Chop the walnuts and dates on your cutting board. Take the baking dish out of the oven and drizzle slices with olive oil.
4. Crack an egg into each of the holes in the slices and season with pepper and salt. Sprinkle the chopped walnuts on top. Bake for 10 minutes more. Garnish with parsley and add maple syrup.

Nutrition:
- Calories: 198.
- Protein: 8 g.
- Fat: 12 g.
- Carbs: 17 g.

27.   Barley Porridge

Preparation Time: 5 minutes.
Cooking Time: 25 minutes.
Servings: 4
Ingredients:
- 1 cup barley.
- 1 cup wheat berries.
- 2 cups unsweetened almond milk.
- 2 cups water.
- ½ cup blueberries.
- ½ cup pomegranate seeds.
- ½ cup hazelnuts, toasted and chopped.
- ¼ cup honey.

Directions:

1. Take a medium saucepan and place it over medium-high heat. Place barley, almond milk, wheat berries, water and bring to a boil. Reduce the heat to low and simmer for 25 minutes.
2. Divide amongst serving bowls and top each serving with 2 tbsp. blueberries, 2 tbsp. pomegranate seeds, 2 tbsp. hazelnuts, 1 tbsp. honey. Serve and enjoy!

Nutrition:
- Calories: 295.Protein: 6 g.
- Fat: 8 g.
- Carbs: 56 g.

28.   Tomato and Dill Frittata

Preparation Time: 5 minutes.
Cooking Time: 10 minutes.
Servings: 4
Ingredients:
- 2 tbsp. olive oil.
- 1 medium onion, chopped.
- 1 tsp. garlic, minced.
- 2 medium tomatoes, chopped.
- 6 large eggs.
- ½ cup half and half.
- ½ cup feta cheese, crumbled.
- ¼ cup dill weed.
- Salt as needed.
- Ground black pepper as needed.

Directions:

1. Pre-heat your oven to a temperature of 400°F. Take a large-sized ovenproof pan and heat up your olive oil over medium-high heat. Toss in the onion, garlic, tomatoes and stir fry them for 4 minutes.
2. While they are being cooked, take a bowl and beat together your eggs, half and half cream, and season the mix with some pepper and salt.
3. Pour the mixture into the pan with your vegetables and top it with crumbled feta cheese and dill weed. Cover it with the lid and let it cook for 3 minutes.
4. Place the pan inside your oven and let it bake for 10 minutes. Serve hot.

Nutrition:
- Calories: 191.
- Protein: 9 g.
- Fat: 15 g.
- Carbs: 6 g.

29.   Strawberry and Rhubarb Smoothie

Preparation Time: 5 minutes.
Cooking Time: 3 minutes.
Servings: 1
Ingredients:
- 1 rhubarb stalk, chopped.
- 1 cup fresh strawberries, sliced.
- ½ cup plain Greek yogurt.
- Pinch ground cinnamon.
- 3 ice cubes.
- Honey.

Directions:

1. Take a small saucepan and fill it with water over high heat. Bring to boil and add rhubarb,

boil for 3 minutes. Drain and transfer to the blender.

2. Add strawberries, honey, yogurt, cinnamon, and pulse mixture until smooth. Add ice cubes and blend until thick with no lumps. Pour into glass and enjoy chilled.

Nutrition:

- Calories: 295.
- Protein: 6 g.
- Fat: 8 g.
- Carbs: 56 g.

30. Bacon and Brie Omelet Wedges

Preparation Time: 10 minutes.
Cooking Time: 10 minutes.
Servings: 6
Ingredients:

- 2 tbsp. olive oil.
- 7 oz. smoked bacon.
- 6 beaten eggs.
- Small bunch chives, snipped.
- 3 ½ oz. brie, sliced.
- 1 tsp. red wine vinegar.
- 1 tsp. Dijon mustard.
- 1 cucumber, halved, deseeded, and sliced diagonally.
- 7 oz. radish, quartered.

Directions:

1. Turn your grill on and set it to high. Take a small-sized pan and add 1 tsp. of oil, allow the oil to heat up. Add lardons and fry until crisp. Drain the lardon on kitchen paper.
2. Take another non-stick cast iron frying pan and place it over the grill, heat 2 tsp. of oil. Add lardons, eggs, chives, ground pepper to the frying pan. Cook on low until they are semi-set.
3. Carefully lay brie on top and grill until the brie sets and is a golden texture. Remove it from the pan and cut it up into wedges.
4. Take a small bowl and create dressing by mixing olive oil, mustard, vinegar, and seasoning. Add cucumber to the bowl and mix, serve alongside the omelet wedges.

Nutrition:

- Calories: 35.
- Protein: 25 g.
- Fat: 31 g.
- Carbs: 3 g.

31. Pearl Couscous Salad

Preparation Time: 15 minutes.
Cooking Time: 0 minutes.
Servings: 6
Ingredients:
For lemon dill vinaigrette:

- 1 large-sized lemon, juice.
- $1/3$ cup extra virgin olive oil.
- 1 tsp. dill weed.
- 1 tsp. garlic powder.
- Salt as needed. - Pepper.

For Israeli couscous:

- 2 cups pearl couscous.
- Extra virgin olive oil.
- 2 cups halved grape tomatoes.
- Water as needed.
- $1/3$ cup finely chopped red onions.
- ½ finely chopped English cucumber.
- 15 oz. chickpeas.
- 14 oz. can artichoke hearts (roughly chopped up).
- ½ cup pitted Klamath olives.
- 15 to 20 pieces fresh basil leaves, roughly torn and chopped up.
- 3 oz. fresh baby mozzarella.

Directions:

1. Prepare the vinaigrette by taking a bowl and add the Ingredients listed under vinaigrette. Mix them well and keep them aside. Take a medium-sized heavy pot and place it over medium heat.
2. Add 2 tbsp. of olive oil and allow it to heat up. Add couscous and keep cooking until golden brown. Add 3 cups of boiling water and cook the couscous according to the package instructions.
3. Once done, drain in a colander and keep aside. Take another large-sized mixing bowl and add the remaining Ingredients except for the cheese and basil.
4. Add the cooked couscous and basil to the mix and mix everything well. Give the vinaigrette a nice stir and whisk it into the couscous salad. Mix well.
5. Adjust the seasoning as required. Add mozzarella cheese. Garnish with some basil. Enjoy!

Nutrition:

- Calories: 393. Protein: 13 g.
- Fat: 13 g. Carbs: 57 g.

32. Coconut Porridge

Preparation Time: 15 minutes.
Cooking Time: 0 minutes.
Servings: 6
Ingredients:

- Powdered erythritol, as needed.
- 1 ½ cups almond milk, unsweetened.
- 2 tbsp. vanilla protein powder.
- 3 tbsp. golden flaxseed meal.
- 2 tbsp. coconut flour.

Directions:
1. Take a bowl and mix in flaxseed meal, protein powder, coconut flour, and mix well. Add mix to the saucepan (placed over medium heat).
2. Add almond milk and stir, let the mixture thicken. Add your desired amount of sweetener and serve. Enjoy!

Nutrition:
- Calories: 259.
- Protein: 16 g.
- Fat: 13 g.
- Carbs: 5 g.

33. Crumbled Feta and Scallions

Preparation Time: 5 minutes.
Cooking Time: 15 minutes.
Servings: 12
Ingredients:

- 2 tbsp. unsalted butter (replace with canola oil for full effect).
- ½ cup chopped-up scallions.
- 1 cup crumbled feta cheese.
- 8 large-sized eggs.
- $^2/_3$ cup milk.
- ½ tsp. dried Italian seasoning.
- Salt as needed.
- Freshly ground black pepper as needed.
- Cooking oil spray.

Directions:
1. Preheat your oven to 400°F. Take a 3-4 oz. muffin pan and grease with cooking oil. Take a non-stick pan and place it over medium heat.
2. Add butter and allow the butter to melt. Add half of the scallions and stir fry. Keep them to the side. Take a medium-sized bowl and add eggs, Italian seasoning, and milk and whisk well.
3. Add the stir-fried scallions and feta cheese and mix. Season with pepper and salt. Pour the mix into the muffin tin. Transfer the muffin tin to your oven and bake for 15 minutes. Serve with a sprinkle of scallions.

Nutrition:
- Calories: 106.
- Protein: 7 g.
- Fat: 8 g.
- Carbs: 2 g.

34. Gnocchi Ham Olives

Preparation Time: 5 minutes.
Cooking Time: 15 minutes.
Servings: 4
Ingredients:

- 2 tbsp. olive oil.
- 1 medium-sized onion chopped up.
- 3 minced garlic cloves.
- 1 medium-sized red pepper completely deseeded and finely chopped.
- 1 cup tomato puree.
- 2 tbsp. tomato paste.
- 1 pound gnocchi.
- 1 cup coarsely chopped turkey ham.
- ½ cup sliced pitted olives.
- 1 tsp. Italian seasoning.
- Salt as needed.
- Freshly ground black pepper.
- Bunch fresh basil leaves.

Directions:
1. Take a medium-sized saucepan and place over medium-high heat. Pour some olive oil and heat it up. Toss in the bell pepper, onion, and garlic and sauté for 2 minutes.
2. Pour in the tomato puree, gnocchi, tomato paste, and add the turkey ham, Italian seasoning, and olives. Simmer the whole mix for 15 minutes, making sure to stir from time to time.

3. Season the mix with some pepper and salt. Once done, transfer the mix to a dish and garnish with some basil leaves. Serve hot and have fun.

Nutrition:
- Calories: 335.
- Protein: 15 g.
- Fat: 12 g.
- Carbs: 45 g.

35. Spicy Early Morning Seafood Risotto

Preparation Time: 5 minutes.
Cooking Time: 15 minutes.
Servings: 4
Ingredients:
- 3 cups clam juice.
- 2 cups water.
- 2 tbsp. olive oil.
- 1 medium-sized chopped-up onion.
- 2 minced garlic cloves.
- 1 ½ cups arborio rice.
- ½ cup dry white wine.
- 1 tsp. saffron.
- ½ tsp. ground cumin.
- ½ tsp. paprika.
- 1 pound marinara seafood mix.
- Salt as needed.
- Ground pepper as needed.

Directions:
1. Place a saucepan over high heat and pour in your clam juice with water and bring the mixture to a boil. Remove the heat.
2. Take a heavy-bottomed saucepan and stir fry your garlic and onion in oil over medium heat until a nice fragrance comes off.
3. Add in the rice and keep stirring for 2 to 3 minutes until the rice has been fully covered with the oil. Pour the wine and then add the saffron.
4. Keep stirring constantly until it is fully absorbed. Add in the cumin, clam juice, paprika mixture 1 cup at a time, making sure to keep stirring it from time to time.
5. Cook the rice for 20 minutes until perfect. Finally, add the seafood marinara mix and cook for another 5 to 7 minutes.
6. Season with some pepper and salt. Transfer the meal to a serving dish. Serve hot.

Nutrition:
- Calories: 386.
- Protein: 21 g.
- Fat: 7 g.
- Carbs: 55 g.

36. Rocket Tomatoes and Mushroom Frittata

Preparation Time: 5 minutes.
Cooking Time: 15 minutes.
Servings: 4
Ingredients:
- 2 tbsp. butter (replace with canola oil for full effect).
- 1 chopped-up medium-sized onion.
- 2 minced garlic cloves.
- 1 cup coarsely chopped baby rocket tomato.
- 1 cup sliced button mushrooms.
- 6 large pieces eggs.
- ½ cup skim milk.
- 1 tsp. dried rosemary.
- Salt as needed.
- Ground black pepper as needed.

Directions:
1. Preheat your oven to 400°F. Take a large oven-proof pan and place it over medium heat. Heat up some oil.
2. Stir fry your garlic, onion for about 2 minutes. Add the mushroom, rosemary, and rockets and cook for 3 minutes. Take a medium-sized bowl and beat your eggs alongside the milk.
3. Season it with some salt and pepper. Pour the egg mixture into your pan with the vegetables and sprinkle some Parmesan.
4. Reduce the heat to low and cover with the lid. Let it cook for 3 minutes. Transfer the pan into your oven and bake for 10 minutes until fully settled.
5. Reduce the heat to low and cover with your lid. Let it cook for 3 minutes. Transfer the pan into your oven and then bake for another 10 minutes. Serve hot.

Nutrition:
- Calories: 189.
- Protein: 12 g.
- Fat: 13 g.
- Carbs: 6 g.

37. Cheesy Olives Bread

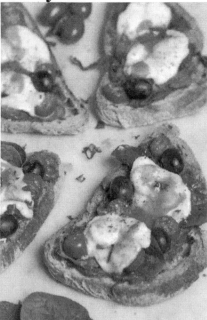

Preparation Time: 1 hour and 40 minutes.

Cooking Time: 30 minutes.

Servings: 10

Ingredients:

- 4 cups whole-wheat flour.
- 3 tbsp. oregano, chopped.
- 2 tsp. dry yeast.
- ¼ cup olive oil.
- 1 ½ cups black olives, pitted and sliced.
- 1 cup water.
- ½ cup feta cheese, crumbled.

Directions:

1. In a bowl, mix the flour with the water, the yeast, and the oil. Stir and knead your dough very well. Put the dough in a bowl, cover with plastic wrap, and keep in a warm place for 1 hour.
2. Divide the dough into 2 bowls and stretch each ball well. Add the rest of the Ingredients to each ball and tuck them inside. Knead the dough well again.
3. Flatten the balls a bit and leave them aside for 40 minutes more. Transfer the balls to a baking sheet lined with parchment paper, make a small slit in each, and bake at 425°F for 30 minutes.
4. Serve the bread as a Mediterranean breakfast.

Nutrition:

- Calories: 251.
- Fat: 7.3 g.
- Carbs: 39.7 g.
- Protein: 6.7 g.

38. Sweet Potato Tart

Preparation Time: 10 minutes.

Cooking Time: 1 hour and 10 minutes.

Servings: 8

Ingredients:

- 2 pounds sweet potatoes, peeled and cubed.
- ¼ cup olive oil + a drizzle.
- 7 oz. feta cheese, crumbled.
- 1 yellow onion, chopped.
- 2 eggs, whisked.
- ¼ cup almond milk.
- 1 tbsp. herbs de Provence.
- A pinch salt and black pepper.
- 6 phyllo sheets.
- 1 tbsp. parmesan, grated.

Directions:

1. In a bowl, combine the potatoes with half of the oil, salt, and pepper, toss, spread on a baking sheet lined with parchment paper, and roast at 400°F for 25 minutes.
2. Meanwhile, heat a pan with half of the remaining oil over medium heat, add the onion, and sauté for 5 minutes.
3. In a bowl, combine the eggs with the milk, feta, herbs, salt, pepper, onion, sweet potatoes, and the rest of the oil and toss.
4. Arrange the phyllo sheets in a tart pan and brush them with a drizzle of oil. Add the sweet potato mix and spread it well into the pan.
5. Sprinkle the parmesan on top and bake covered with tin foil at 350°F for 20 minutes. Remove the tin foil, bake the tart for 20 minutes more, cool it down, slice, and serve for breakfast.

Nutrition:

- Calories: 476.
- Fat: 16.8 g.
- Carbs: 68.8 g.
- Protein: 13.9 g.

39. Stuffed Pita Breads

Preparation Time: 5 minutes.

Cooking Time: 15 minutes.

Servings: 4

Ingredients:

- 1 ½ tbsp. olive oil.
- 1 tomato, cubed.
- 1 garlic clove, minced.
- 1 red onion, chopped.
- ¼ cup parsley, chopped.
- 15 oz. canned fava beans, drained and rinsed.

- ¼ cup lemon juice.
- Salt and black pepper to the taste.
- 4 whole-wheat pita bread pockets.

Directions:

1. Heat a pan with the oil over medium heat; add the onion, stir, and sauté for 5 minutes. Add the rest of the Ingredients, stir, and cook for 10 minutes more
2. Stuff the pita pockets with this mix and serve for breakfast.

Nutrition:

- Calories: 382.
- Protein: 28.5 g.
- Fat: 1.8 g.
- Carbs: 66 g.

40. Blueberries Quinoa

Preparation Time: 5 minutes.
Cooking Time: 0 minutes.
Servings: 4
Ingredients:

- 2 cups almond milk.
- 2 cups quinoa, already cooked.
- ½ tsp. cinnamon powder.
- 1 tbsp. honey.
- 1 cup blueberries.
- ¼ cup walnuts, chopped.

Directions:

1. In a bowl, mix the quinoa with the milk and the rest of the Ingredients, toss, divide into smaller bowls and serve for breakfast.

Nutrition:

- Calories: 284.
- Protein: 4.4 g.
- Fat: 14.3 g.
- Carbs: 15.4 g.

CHAPTER 11:

Beef, Pork and Lamb Recipes

41. Soy Sauce Beef Roast

Preparation Time: 8 minutes.
Cooking Time: 35 minutes.
Servings: 2
Ingredients:

- ½ tsp. beef bouillon.
- 1 ½ tsp. rosemary.
- ½ tsp. minced garlic.
- 2 pounds roast beef.
- $^1/_3$ cup soy sauce.

Directions:

1. Combine the soy sauce, bouillon, rosemary, and garlic together in a mixing bowl.
2. Turn on your instant pot. Place the roast, and pour enough water to cover the roast; gently stir to mix well. Seal it tight.
3. Click "MEAT/STEW" Cooking function; set pressure level to "HIGH" and set the Cooking Time to 35 minutes. Let the pressure build to cook the Ingredients. Once done, click the "CANCEL" setting then click the "NPR" Cooking function to release the pressure naturally.
4. Gradually open the lid, and shred the meat. Mix in the shredded meat back in the potting mix and stir well. Transfer in serving containers. Serve warm.

Nutrition:

- Calories: 423.
- Protein: 21 g.
- Fat: 14 g.
- Sodium: 884 mg.
- Carbs: 12 g.

42. Slow Cooker Meatloaf

Preparation Time: 10 minutes.
Cooking Time: 6 hours and 10 minutes.
Servings: 2
Ingredients:

- 2 pounds ground bison.

- 1 grated zucchini.
- 2 large eggs.
- Olive oil cooking spray, as required.
- 1 zucchini, shredded.
- ½ cup parsley, fresh, finely chopped.
- ½ cup parmesan cheese, shredded.
- 3 tbsp. balsamic vinegar.
- 4 garlic cloves, grated.
- 2 tbsp. onion minced.
- 1 tbsp. dried oregano.
- ½ tsp. ground black pepper.
- ½ tsp. kosher salt.

For the topping:

- ¼ cup shredded mozzarella cheese.
- ¼ cup ketchup without Sugar.
- ¼ cup freshly chopped parsley.

Directions:

1. Stripe line the inside of a six-quart slow cooker with aluminum foil. Spray non-stick cooking oil over it.
2. In a large bowl combine ground bison or extra lean ground sirloin, zucchini, eggs, parsley, balsamic vinegar, garlic, dried oregano, sea or kosher salt, minced dry onion, and ground black pepper.
3. Situate this mixture into the slow cooker and form an oblong-shaped loaf. Cover the cooker, set on low heat, and cook for 6 hours. After cooking, open the cooker and spread ketchup all over the meatloaf.
4. Now, place the cheese above the ketchup as a new layer and close the slow cooker. Let the meatloaf sit on these two layers for about 10 minutes or until the cheese starts to melt. Garnish with fresh parsley and shredded mozzarella cheese.

Nutrition:

- Calories: 320.
- Protein: 26 g.
- Fat: 2 g.
- Sodium: 681 mg.
- Carbs: 4 g.

43. Simple Pork Stir Fry

Preparation Time: 10 minutes.
Cooking Time: 15 minutes.
Servings: 4
Ingredients:

- 4 oz. bacon, chopped.
- 4 oz. snow peas.
- 2 tbsp. butter.

- 1-pound pork loin, cut into thin strips.
- 2 cups mushrooms, sliced.
- ¾ cup white wine.
- ½ cup yellow onion, chopped.
- 3 tbsp. sour cream.
- Salt and white pepper to taste.

Directions:

1. Put snow peas in a saucepan, add water to cover, add a pinch of salt, bring to a boil over medium heat, cook until they are soft, drain and leave aside.
2. Heat a pan over medium-high heat, add bacon, cook for a few minutes, drain grease, transfer to a bowl and leave aside.
3. Heat a pan with 1 tbsp. of butter over medium heat, add pork strips, salt, and pepper to taste, brown for a few minutes, and transfer to a plate as well.
4. Return pan to medium heat, add remaining butter and melt it. Add onions and mushrooms, stir and cook for 4 minutes.
5. Add wine, and simmer until it's reduced. Add cream, peas, pork, salt, and pepper to taste, stir, heat up, divide between plates, top with bacon, and serve.

Nutrition:

- Calories: 343.
- Protein: 23 g.
- Fat: 31 g.
- Carbs: 21 g.

44. Pork and Chickpea Stew

Preparation Time: 20 minutes.
Cooking Time: 8 hours.
Servings: 4
Ingredients:

- 2 tbsp. white flour.
- ½ cup chicken stock.
- 1 tbsp. ginger, grated.

- 1 tsp. coriander, ground.
- 2 tsp. cumin, ground.
- Salt and black pepper to taste.
- 2 ½ pounds pork butt, cubed.
- 28 oz. canned tomatoes, drained and chopped.
- 4 oz. carrots, chopped.
- 1 red onion cut in wedges.
- 4 garlic cloves, minced.
- ½ cup apricots, cut in quarters.
- 1 cup couscous, cooked.
- 15 oz. canned chickpeas, drained.
- Cilantro, chopped for serving.

Directions:

1. Put stock in your slow cooker. Add flour, cumin, ginger, coriander, salt, and pepper and stir. Add tomatoes, pork, carrots, garlic, onion, and apricots, cover the cooker and cook on Low for 7 hours and 50 minutes.
2. Add chickpeas and couscous, cover, and cook for 10 more minutes. Divide on plates, sprinkle cilantro and serve right away.

Nutrition:

- Calories: 216.
- Protein: 23 g.
- Fat: 31 g.
- Carbs: 21 g.

45. Slow Cooker Mediterranean Beef With Artichokes

Preparation Time: 3 hours and 20 minutes.
Cooking Time: 7 hours and 8 minutes.
Servings: 2
Ingredients:

- 2 pounds beef for stew.
- 14 oz. artichoke hearts.
- 1 tbsp. grapeseed oil.
- 1 diced onion.
- 32 oz. beef broth.
- 4 garlic cloves, grated.
- 14 ½ oz. tinned tomatoes, diced.
- 15 oz. tomato sauce.
- 1 tsp. dried oregano.
- ½ cup pitted chopped olives.
- 1 tsp. dried parsley.
- 1 tsp. dried oregano.
- ½ tsp. ground cumin.
- 1 tsp. dried basil.
- 1 bay leaf.
- ½ tsp. salt.

Directions:

1. In a large non-stick skillet pour some oil and bring to medium-high heat. Roast the beef until it turns brown on both sides. Transfer the beef into a slow cooker.

Nutrition:

- Calories: 314.
- Protein: 32 g.
- Fat: 19 g.
- Sodium: 778 mg.
- Carbs: 1 g.

46. Pork and Greens Salad

Preparation Time: 10 minutes.

Cooking Time: 15 minutes.

Servings: 4

Ingredients:

- 1-pound pork chops, boneless and cut into strips.
- 8 oz. white mushrooms, sliced.
- ½ cup Italian dressing.
- 6 cups mixed salad greens.
- 6 oz. jarred artichoke hearts, drained.
- Salt and black pepper to the taste.
- ½ cup basil, chopped.
- 1 tbsp. olive oil.

Directions:

1. Heat a pan with the oil over medium-high heat, add the pork, and brown for 5 minutes. Add the mushrooms, stir and sauté for 5 minutes more.
2. Add the dressing, artichokes, salad greens, salt, pepper, and basil, cook for 4 to 5 minutes, divide everything into bowls and serve.

Nutrition:

- Calories: 320.
- Protein: 23 g.
- Fat: 31 g.
- Carbs: 21 g.

47. Pork Strips and Rice

Preparation Time: 10 minutes.

Cooking Time: 25 minutes.

Servings: 4

Ingredients:

- ½ pound pork loin, cut into strips.
- Salt and black pepper to taste.
- 2 tbsp. olive oil.
- 2 carrots, chopped.
- 1 red bell pepper, chopped.
- 3 garlic cloves, minced.

- 2 cups veggie stock.
- 1 cup basmati rice.
- ½ cup garbanzo beans.
- 10 black olives, pitted and sliced.
- 1 tbsp. parsley, chopped.

Directions:

1. Heat a pan with the oil over medium-high heat. Add the pork fillets, stir, cook for 5 minutes and transfer them to a plate.
2. Add the carrots, bell pepper, and garlic, stir and cook for 5 more minutes.
3. Add the rice, the stock, beans, and the olives, stir, cook for 14 minutes, divide between plates, sprinkle the parsley on top, and serve.

Nutrition:

- Calories: 220.
- Protein: 23 g.
- Fat: 31 g.
- Carbs: 21 g.

48. Slow-Cooked Mediterranean Pork

Preparation Time: 20 hours and 10 minutes.

Cooking Time: 8 hours.

Servings: 6

Ingredients:

- 3 pounds pork shoulder, boneless.
- ¼ cup olive oil.
- 2 tsp. oregano, dried.
- ¼ cup lemon juice.
- 2 tsp. mustard.
- 2 tsp. mint, chopped.
- 3 garlic cloves, minced.
- 2 tsp. pesto sauce.
- Salt and black pepper to taste.

Directions:

1. In a bowl, mix olive oil with lemon juice, oregano, mint, mustard, garlic, pesto, salt, and pepper then whisk well.
2. Rub pork with marinade, cover, and keep in a cold place for 10 hours. Flip pork shoulder and leave aside for 10 more hours.
3. Transfer to your slow cooker along with the marinade juices, cover, and cook on low for 8 hours. Uncover, slice, divide between plates and serve.

Nutrition:

- Calories: 320.
- Protein: 23 g.
- Fat: 31 g.
- Carbs: 21 g.

49.   Pork and Bean Stew

Preparation Time: 20 minutes.

Cooking Time: 4 hours.

Servings: 4

Ingredients:

- 2 pounds pork neck.
- 1 tbsp. white flour.
- 1 ½ tbsp. olive oil.
- 2 eggplants, chopped.
- 1 brown onion, chopped.
- 1 red bell pepper, chopped.
- 3 garlic cloves, minced.
- 1 tbsp. thyme, dried.
- 2 tsp. sage, dried.
- 4 oz. canned white beans, drained.
- 1 cup chicken stock.
- 12 oz. zucchinis, chopped.
- Salt and pepper to taste.
- 2 tbsp. tomato paste.

Directions:

1. In a bowl, mix flour with salt, pepper, pork neck, and toss. Heat a pan with 2 tsp. pf oil over medium-high heat, add pork and cook for 3 minutes on each side.
2. Transfer pork to a slow cooker and leave aside. Heat the remaining oil in the same pan over medium heat, add eggplant, onion, bell pepper, thyme, sage, and garlic, stir and cook for 5 minutes.
3. Add reserved flour, stir and cook for 1 more minute. Add to pork, then add beans, stock, tomato paste, and zucchinis. Cover and cook on high for 4 hours. Uncover, transfer to plates and serve.

Nutrition:

- Calories: 310. Protein: 23 g.
- Fat: 31 g.
- Carbs: 21 g.

50.   Pork With Couscous

Preparation Time: 10 minutes.

Cooking Time: 7 hours.

Servings: 6

Ingredients:

- 2 ½ pounds pork loin boneless and trimmed.
- ¾ cup chicken stock.
- 2 tbsp. olive oil.
- ½ tbsp. sweet paprika.
- 2 ¼ tsp. sage, dried.
- ½ tbsp. garlic powder.
- ¼ tsp. rosemary, dried.
- ¼ tsp. marjoram, dried.
- 1 tsp. basil, dried.
- 1 tsp. oregano, dried.
- Salt and black pepper to taste.
- 2 cups couscous, cooked.

Directions:

1. In a bowl, mix oil with stock, paprika, garlic powder, sage, rosemary, thyme, marjoram, oregano, salt, and pepper to taste and whisk well. Put pork loin in your crockpot.
2. Add stock and spice mix, stir, cover, and cook on Low for 7 hours. Slice pork return to pot and toss with cooking juices. Divide between plates and serve with couscous on the side.

Nutrition:

- Calories: 320. Protein: 23 g.
- Fat: 31 g.
- Carbs: 21 g.

51.   Grilled Steak, Mushroom, and Onion Kebabs

Preparation Time: 10 minutes.

Cooking Time: 10 minutes.

Servings: 2

Ingredients:

- 1 pound boneless top sirloin steak.
- 8 oz. white button mushrooms.
- 1 medium red onion.
- 4 peeled garlic cloves.
- 2 rosemary sprigs.
- 2 tbsp. extra-virgin olive oil.
- ¼ tsp. black pepper.
- 2 tbsp. red wine vinegar.
- ¼ tsp. sea salt.

Directions:

1. Soak 12 (10-inch) wooden skewers in water. Spray the cold grill with nonstick cooking spray, and heat the grill to medium-high.

2. Cut a piece of aluminum foil into a 10-inch square. Place the garlic and rosemary sprigs in the center, drizzle with 1 tbsp. of oil, and wrap tightly to form a foil packet.
3. Arrange it on the grill, and seal the grill cover.
4. Cut the steak into 1-inch cubes. Thread the beef onto the wet skewers, alternating with whole mushrooms and onion wedges. Spray the kebabs thoroughly with nonstick cooking spray, and sprinkle with pepper.
5. Cook the kebabs on the covered grill for 5 minutes.
6. Flip and grill for 5 more minutes while covered.
7. Unwrap foil packets with garlic and rosemary sprigs and put them into a small bowl.
8. Carefully strip the rosemary sprigs of their leaves into the bowl and pour in any accumulated juices and oil from the foil packet.
9. Mix in the remaining 1 tbsp. of oil and vinegar and salt.
10. Mash the garlic with a fork, and mix all Ingredients in the bowl together. Pour over the finished steak kebabs and serve.

Nutrition:
- Calories: 410.
- Protein: 36 g.
- Fat: 14 g.
- Carbs: 12 g.

52. Cauliflower Steaks With Eggplant Relish

Preparation Time: 5 minutes.
Cooking Time: 25 minutes.
Servings: 2
Ingredients:
- 2 small heads cauliflower (about 3 pounds).
- ¼ tsp. kosher or sea salt.
- ¼ tsp. smoked paprika.
- Extra-virgin olive oil, divided.

Directions:
1. Place a large, rimmed baking sheet in the oven. Preheat the oven to 400°F with the pan inside.
2. Stand one head of cauliflower on a cutting board, stem-end down. With a long chef's knife, slice down through the very center of the head, including the stem.
3. Starting at the cut edge, measure about 1 inch and cut one thick slice from each cauliflower half, including as much of the stem as possible, to make two cauliflower "steaks."

4. Reserve the remaining cauliflower for another use. Repeat with the second cauliflower head.
5. Dry each steak well with a clean towel. Sprinkle the salt and smoked paprika evenly over both sides of each cauliflower steak.
6. In a large skillet over medium-high heat, heat 2 tbsp. of oil. When the oil is very hot, add two cauliflower steaks to the pan and cook for about 3 minutes, until golden and crispy. Flip and cook for 2 more minutes.
7. Transfer the steaks to a plate. Use a pair of tongs to hold a paper towel and wipe out the pan to remove most of the hot oil (which will contain a few burnt bits of cauliflower).
8. Repeat the cooking process with the remaining 2 tbsp. of oil and the remaining two steaks.
9. Using oven mitts, carefully remove the baking sheet from the oven and place the cauliflower on the baking sheet.
10. Roast in the oven for 12 to 15 minutes, until the cauliflower steaks are just forked tender; they will still be somewhat firm. Serve the steaks with the eggplant relish spread, baba ghanoush, or homemade ketchup.

Nutrition:
- Calories: 206.
- Protein: 8 g.
- Fat: 17 g.
- Carbs: 3 g.

53. Tasty Lamb Leg

Preparation Time: 10 minutes.
Cooking Time: 20 minutes.
Servings: 2
Ingredients:
- 2 lbs. leg lamb, boneless and cut into chunks.
- 1 tbsp. olive oil.
- 1 tbsp. garlic, sliced.
- 1 cup red wine.
- 1 cup onion, chopped.
- 2 carrots, chopped.
- 1 tsp. rosemary, chopped.
- 2 tsp. thyme, chopped.
- 1 tsp. oregano, chopped.
- ½ cup beef stock.
- 2 tbsp. tomato paste.
- Pepper.
- Salt.

Directions:
1. Add oil into the inner pot of the instant pot and set the pot on sauté mode.

2. Add meat and sauté until browned.
3. Add remaining Ingredients and stir well.
4. Seal pot with lid and cook on high for 15 minutes.
5. Once done, allow to release pressure naturally. Remove lid.
6. Stir well and serve.

Nutrition:
- Calories: 540. Protein: 65.2 g.
- Fat: 20.4 g. Sugar: 4.2 g.
- Cholesterol: 204 mg.
- Carbs: 10.3 g.

54. Kale Sprouts & Lamb

Preparation Time: 10 minutes.
Cooking Time: 30 minutes.
Servings: 2
Ingredients:
- 2 pounds lamb, cut into chunks.
- 1 tbsp. parsley, chopped.
- 2 tbsp. olive oil.
- 1 cup kale, chopped.
- 1 cup brussels sprouts, halved.
- 1 cup beef stock.
- ½ tbsp Pepper.
- A pinch of Salt.

Directions:
1. Add all Ingredients into the inner pot of the instant pot and stir well.
2. Seal pot with lid and cook on high for 30 minutes.
3. Once done, allow to release pressure naturally. Remove lid.
4. Serve and enjoy.

Nutrition:
- Calories: 504. Protein: 65.7 g.
- Fat: 23.8 g. Sugar: 0.5 g.
- Cholesterol: 204 mg.
- Carbs: 3.9 g.

55. Mediterranean Lamb Chops

Preparation Time: 10 minutes.
Cooking Time: 10 minutes.
Servings: 2
Ingredients:
- 4 lamb shoulder chops, 8 oz. each.
- 2 tbsp. Dijon mustard.
- 2 tbsp. balsamic vinegar.
- 1 tbsp. garlic, chopped.
- ½ cup olive oil.
- 2 tbsp. shredded fresh basil.

Directions:
1. Pat your lamb chop dry using a kitchen towel and arrange them on a shallow glass baking dish.
2. Take a bowl and whisk in Dijon mustard, balsamic vinegar, garlic, pepper, and mix well.
3. Whisk in the oil very slowly into the marinade until the mixture is smooth.
4. Stir in basil.
5. Pour the marinade over the lamb chops and stir to coat both sides well.
6. Cover the chops and allow them to marinate for 1 to 4 hours (chilled).
7. Take the chops out and leave them for 30 minutes to allow the temperature to reach the normal level.
8. Preheat your grill to medium heat and add oil to the grate.
9. Grill the lamb chops for 5 to 10 minutes per side until both sides are browned.
10. Once the center of the chop reads 145°F, the chops are ready, serve and enjoy!

Nutrition:
- Calories: 521.
- Protein: 22 g.
- Fat: 45 g.
- Carbs: 3.5 g.

56. Mushroom and Beef Risotto

Preparation Time: 5 minutes.
Cooking Time: 10 minutes.
Servings: 2
Ingredients:
- 2 cups low-Sodium beef stock.
- 2 cups water.
- 2 tbsp. olive oil.
- ½ cup scallions, chopped.
- 1 cup arborio rice.
- ¼ cup dry white wine.
- 1 cup roast beef, thinly stripped.

- 1 cup button mushrooms.
- ½ cup canned cream mushroom.
- Salt and pepper as needed.
- Oregano, chopped.
- Parsley, chopped.

Directions:

1. Take a stock pot and put it over medium heat.
2. Add water with beef stock in it.
3. Bring the mixture to a boil and remove the heat.
4. Take another heavy-bottomed saucepan and put it over medium heat.
5. Add in the scallions and stir fry them for 1 minute.
6. Add in the rice then and cook it for at least 2 minutes, occasionally stirring it to ensure that it is finely coated with oil.
7. In the rice mixture, keep adding your beef stock ½ a cup at a time, making sure to stir it often.
8. Once all the stock has been added, cook the rice for another 2 minutes.
9. During the last 5 minutes of your cooking, make sure to add the beef, cream of the mushroom while stirring it nicely.
10. Transfer the whole mix to a serving dish.
11. Garnish with some chopped-up parsley and oregano. Serve hot.

Nutrition:

- Calories: 378.
- Protein: 23 g.
- Fat: 12 g.
- Carbs: 41 g.

57. Balearic Beef Brisket Bowl

Preparation Time: 0 minutes.
Cooking Time: 50 minutes.
Servings: 2
Ingredients:

- ½ cup Manto negro dry red wine (Spanish or Mallorca dry red wine).
- $1/3$ cup olives, pitted and chopped.
- 14.5 oz. tomatoes with juice (diced).
- 5 garlic cloves, chopped.
- ½ tsp. dried rosemary.
- Salt and pepper.
- 2 ½ pounds beef brisket.
- Olive oil.
- 1 tbsp. fresh parsley, finely chopped.
- 1 ½ cups sautéed green beans.

Directions:

1. Pour the dry wine and olives in your slow cooker, and stir in the tomatoes, garlic, and rosemary.
2. Sprinkle salt and pepper to taste over the beef brisket. Place the seasoned meat on top of the wine-tomato mixture. Ladle half of the mixture over the meat. Cover the slow cooker and cook for 6 hours on high heat until fork-tender.
3. Transfer the cooked brisket to a chopping board. Tent the meat with foil and let stand for 10 minutes.
4. Drizzle with olive oil. Cut the brisket into 6-slices across its grain. Transfer the slices to a serving platter, and spoon some sauce over the meat slices. Sprinkle with parsley.
5. Serve with sautéed green beans and the remaining sauce.

Nutrition:

- Calories: 370.
- Protein: 41 g.
- Fats: 18 g.
- Dietary Fiber: 1 g.
- Carbs: 6 g.

58. Mediterranean Beef Skewers

Preparation Time: 5 minutes.
Cooking Time: 8 minutes.
Servings: 2
Ingredients:

- 2 pounds cubed beef sirloin.
- 3 minced garlic cloves.
- 1 tbsp. fresh lemon zest.
- 1 tbsp. chopped parsley.
- 2 tsp. chopped thyme.
- 2 tsp. minced rosemary.
- 2 tsp. dried oregano.
- 4 tbsp. olive oil.
- 2 tbsp. fresh lemon juice.
- Sea salt and ground black pepper, to taste.

Directions:

1. Add all the Ingredients, except the beef, to a bowl.
2. Preheat the grill to medium-high heat.
3. Mix in the beef to marinate for 1 hour.
4. Arrange the marinated beef onto skewers then cook on the preheated grill for 8 minutes flipping occasionally.

5. Once cooked, leave aside to rest for 5 minutes then serve.

Nutrition:

- Calories: 370.
- Fats: 46 g.
- Protein: 60 g.
- Carbs: 12 g.

59. Cumin Lamb Mix

Preparation Time: 15 minutes.

Cooking Time: 10 minutes.

Servings: 2

Ingredients:

- 2 lamb chops (3.5 oz. each).
- 1 tbsp. olive oil.
- 1 tsp. ground cumin.
- ½ tsp. salt.

Directions:

1. Rub the lamb chops with ground cumin and salt. Then sprinkle them with olive oil. Let the meat marinate for 10 minutes. After this, preheat the skillet well.
2. Place the lamb chops in the skillet and roast them for 10 minutes. Flip the meat on another side from time to time to avoid burning.

Nutrition:

- Calories: 384.
- Protein: 19.2 g.
- Fat: 33.2 g.
- Carbs: 0.5 g.

60. Beef & Potatoes

Preparation Time: 15 minutes.

Cooking Time: 20 minutes.

Servings: 6

Ingredients:

- 1 ½ pound stew beef, sliced into cubes.
- 2 tsp. mixed dried herbs (thyme, sage).
- 4 potatoes, cubed.

- 10 oz. mushrooms.
- 1 ½ cups red wine.

Directions:

1. Set the Instant Pot to sauté. Add 1 tbsp. of olive oil and cook the beef until brown on all sides. Add the rest of the Ingredients.
2. Season with salt and pepper. Pour 1 ½ cups water into the pot. Mix well. Cover the pot. Set it to manual. Cook at high pressure for 20 minutes. Release the pressure naturally.

Nutrition:

- Calories: 360.
- Protein: 29.9 g.
- Fat: 9.6 g.
- Carbs: 29.3 g.

61. Pork and Chestnuts Mix

Preparation Time: 15 minutes.

Cooking Time: 0 minutes.

Servings: 6

Ingredients:

- 1 ½ cups brown rice, already cooked.
- 2 cups pork roast, already cooked and shredded.
- 3 oz. water chestnuts, drained and sliced.
- ½ cup sour cream.
- A pinch salt and white pepper.

Directions:

1. In a bowl, mix the rice with the roast and the other Ingredients, toss and keep in the fridge for 2 hours before serving.

Nutrition:

- Calories: 294.
- Protein: 23.5 g.
- Fat: 17 g.
- Carbs: 16 g.

62. Rosemary Pork Chops

Preparation Time: 15 minutes.

Cooking Time: 25 minutes.

Servings: 4

Ingredients:

- 4 pork loin chops, boneless.
- Salt and black pepper to the taste.
- 4 garlic cloves, minced.
- 1 tbsp. rosemary, chopped.
- 1 tbsp. olive oil.

Directions:

1. In a roasting pan, combine the pork chops with the rest of the Ingredients, toss, and bake at 425°F for 10 minutes.

2. Reduce the heat to 350°F and cook the chops for 25 minutes more. Divide the chops between plates and serve with a side salad.

Nutrition:
- Calories: 161.
- Protein: 25 g.
- Fat: 5 g.
- Carbs: 1 g.

63.   Tender Lamb

Preparation Time: 45 minutes.
Cooking Time: 40 minutes.
Servings: 6
Ingredients:
- 3 lamb shanks.
- Seasoning mixture (1 tbsp. oregano, ¼ tsp. ground cumin, and 1 tbsp. smoked paprika).
- 3 garlic cloves, minced.
- 2 cups red wine.
- 4 cups beef stock.
- Salt and pepper, to taste.
- Olive oil.

Directions:
1. Coat the lamb shanks with the seasoning mixture. Sprinkle with salt and pepper. Cover with minced garlic. Marinate in half of the mixture for 30 minutes.
2. Set the Instant Pot to sauté. Pour in 2 tbsp. of olive oil. Brown the lamb on all sides. Remove and set aside. Add the rest of the Ingredients.
3. Put the lamb back in the pot. Cover the pot and set it to manual. Cook at high pressure for 30 minutes. Release the pressure naturally. Set the Instant Pot to sauté to simmer and thicken the sauce.

Nutrition:
- Calories: 566.
- Protein: 48.7 g.
- Fat: 29.4 g.
- Carbs: 12 g.

64.   Worcestershire Pork Chops

Preparation Time: 15 minutes.
Cooking Time: 15 minutes.
Servings: 3
Ingredients:
- 2 tbsp. Worcestershire sauce.
- 8 oz. pork loin chops.
- 1 tbsp. lemon juice.
- 1 tsp. olive oil.

Directions:
1. Mix up together Worcestershire sauce, lemon juice, and olive oil. Brush the pork loin chops with the sauce mixture from each side. Preheat the grill to 395°F.
2. Place the pork chops in the grill and cook them for 5 minutes. Then flip the pork chops on another side and brush with the remaining sauce mixture. Grill the meat for 7 to 8 minutes more.

Nutrition:
- Calories: 267.
- Protein: 17 g.
- Fat: 20.4 g.
- Carbs: 2.1 g.

65.   Greek Pork

Preparation Time: 15 minutes.
Cooking Time: 50 minutes.
Servings: 8
Ingredients:
- 3 pounds pork roast, sliced into cubes.
- ¼ cup chicken broth.
- ¼ cup lemon juice.
- 2 tsp. dried oregano.
- 2 tsp. garlic powder.

Directions:
1. Put the pork in the Instant Pot. In a bowl, mix all the remaining Ingredients. Pour the mixture over the pork. Toss to coat evenly. Secure the pot.
2. Choose a manual mode. Cook at high pressure for 50 minutes. Release the pressure naturally.

Nutrition:
- Calories: 478.
- Protein: 65.1 g.
- Fat: 21.6 g.
- Carbs: 1.2 g.

66. Pork With Green Beans & Potatoes

Preparation Time: 15 minutes.

Cooking Time: 22 minutes

Servings: 6

Ingredients:

- 1 pound lean pork, sliced into cubes.
- 1 onion, chopped.
- 2 carrots, sliced thinly.
- 2 cups canned crushed tomatoes.
- 2 potatoes, cubed.

Directions:

1. Set the Instant Pot to sauté. Add ½ cup of olive oil. Cook the pork for 5 minutes, stirring frequently. Add the rest of the Ingredients. Mix well.
2. Seal the pot. Choose a manual setting. Cook at high pressure for 17 minutes. Release the pressure naturally.

Nutrition:

- Calories: 428.
- Protein: 26.7 g.
- Fat: 24.4 g.
- Carbs: 27.6 g.

67. Beef and Chili Mix

Preparation Time: 15 minutes.

Cooking Time: 16 minutes.

Servings: 4

Ingredients:

- 2 green chili peppers.
- 8 oz. beef flank steak.
- 1 tsp. salt.
- 2 tbsp. olive oil.
- 1 tsp. apple cider vinegar.

Directions:

1. Pour olive oil into the skillet. Place the flank steak in the oil and roast it for 3 minutes from each side. Then sprinkle the meat with salt and apple cider vinegar.
2. Chop the chili peppers and add them to the skillet. Fry the beef for 10 minutes more. Stir it from time to time.

Nutrition:

- Calories:166.
- Protein: 17.2 g.
- Fat: 10.5 g.
- Carbs: 0.2 g.

68. Greek Meatballs

Preparation Time: 15 minutes.

Cooking Time: 10 minutes.

Servings: 8 to 10

Ingredients:

- 2 pounds ground lamb.
- 1 onion, chopped.
- ¼ cup fresh parsley, chopped.
- ½ cup almond flour.
- 1 tsp. dried oregano.

Directions:

1. In a large bowl, combine all the Ingredients. Mix well and form into small meatballs. Put the balls on the steamer basket inside the Instant Pot.
2. Pour in 1 cup of broth to the bottom of the pot. Secure the pot. Choose manual. Cook at high pressure for 10 minutes. Release the pressure quickly. While waiting, mix the rest of the Ingredients.

Nutrition:

- Calories: 214.
- Protein: 28.7 g.
- Fat: 7.9 g.
- Carbs: 5.5 g.

69. Mediterranean Lamb Bowl

Preparation Time: 15 minutes.

Cooking Time: 15 minutes.

Servings: 2

Ingredients:

- 2 tbsp. extra-virgin olive oil.
- ¼ cup diced yellow onion.
- 1 pound ground lamb.
- 1 tsp. dried mint.
- 1 tsp. dried parsley.
- ½ tsp. red pepper flakes.
- ¼ tsp. garlic powder.
- 1 cup cooked rice.
- ½ tsp. za'atar seasoning.
- ½ cup halved cherry tomatoes.
- 1 cucumber, peeled and diced.
- 1 cup store-bought hummus or garlic-lemon hummus.
- 1 cup crumbled feta cheese.
- 2 pita pieces of bread, warmed (optional).

Directions:

1. In a large sauté pan or skillet, heat the olive oil over medium heat and cook the onion for about 2 minutes, until fragrant.

2. Add the lamb and mix well, breaking up the meat as you cook. Once the lamb is halfway cooked, add mint, parsley, red pepper flakes, and garlic powder.

3. In a medium bowl, mix together the cooked rice and za'atar, then divide between individual serving bowls. Add the seasoned lamb, then top the bowls with the tomatoes, cucumber, hummus, feta, and pita (if using).

Nutrition:

- Calories: 1,312.
- Protein: 62 g.
- Fat: 96 g.
- Carbs: 62 g.

70. Lamb Burger

Preparation Time: 15 minutes.
Cooking Time: 15 minutes.
Servings: 4
Ingredients:

- 1 pound ground lamb.
- ½ small red onion, grated.
- 1 tbsp. dried parsley.
- 1 tsp. dried oregano.
- 1 tsp. ground cumin.
- 1 tsp. garlic powder.
- ½ tsp. dried mint.
- ¼ tsp. paprika.
- ¼ tsp. kosher salt.
- $1/_8$ tsp. freshly ground black pepper.
- Extra-virgin olive oil, for panfrying.
- 4 pita pieces of bread, for serving (optional).
- Tzatziki sauce, for serving (optional).
- Pickled onions, for serving (optional).

Directions:

1. In a bowl, combine the lamb, onion, parsley, oregano, cumin, garlic powder, mint, paprika, salt, and pepper. Divide the meat into 4 small balls and work into smooth discs.

2. In a large sauté pan or skillet, heat a drizzle of olive oil over medium heat or brush a grill with oil and set it to medium.

3. Cook the patties for 4 to 5 minutes on each side, until cooked through and juices run clear. Enjoy lamb burgers in pitas, topped with tzatziki sauce and pickled onions (if using).

Nutrition:

- Calories: 328. Protein: 19 g.
- Fat: 27 g. Carbs: 2 g.

71. Quick Herbed Lamb and Pasta

Preparation Time: 15 minutes.
Cooking Time: 15 minutes.
Servings: 4
Ingredients:

- 3 thick lamb sausages, removed from casing and crumbled.
- 1 medium shallot, chopped.
- 1 ½ cups diced baby portobello mushrooms.
- 1 tsp. garlic powder.
- 1 tbsp. extra-virgin olive oil.
- 1 pound bean-based penne pasta.
- 4 medium Roma tomatoes, chopped.
- 1 (14.5 oz.) can crushed tomatoes.
- 3 tbsp. heavy cream.

Directions:

1. Heat a large sauté pan or skillet over medium-high heat. Add the sausage to the skillet and cook for about 5 minutes, mixing and breaking the sausage up until the sausage is halfway cooked.

2. Reduce the heat to medium-low and add the shallot. Continue cooking for about 3 minutes, until they're soft.

3. Add the mushrooms, garlic powder, and olive oil and cook for 5 to 7 minutes, until the mushrooms have reduced in size by half and all the water is cooked out.

4. Meanwhile, bring a large pot of water to a boil and cook the pasta according to the package Directions, until al dente. Drain and set aside.

5. To the skillet, add the chopped and canned tomatoes and cook for 7 to 10 minutes, until the liquid thickens slightly.

6. Reduce the heat and add the cream, mixing well. Plate the pasta first and top with the sausage mixture.

Nutrition:

- Calories: 706. Protein: 45 g.
- Fat: 31 g. Carbs: 79 g.

72. Marinated Lamb Kebabs With Crunchy Yogurt Dressing

Preparation Time: 15 minutes.
Cooking Time: 15 minutes.
Servings: 4
Ingredients:

- ½ cup plain, unsweetened, full-Fat Greek yogurt.
- ¼ cup extra-virgin olive oil.
- ¼ cup freshly squeezed lemon juice.
- 1 tsp. grated lemon zest.
- 2 garlic cloves, minced.
- 2 tbsp. honey.
- 2 tbsp. balsamic vinegar.
- 1 ½ tsp. oregano, fresh, minced.
- 1 tsp. thyme, fresh, minced.
- 1 bay leaf.
- 1 tsp. kosher salt.
- ½ tsp. freshly ground black pepper.
- ½ tsp. red pepper flakes.
- 2 pounds leg lamb, trimmed, cleaned, and cut into 1-inch pieces.
- 1 large red onion, diced largely.
- 1 recipe crunchy yogurt dip.
- Parsley, chopped, for garnish.
- Lemon wedges, for garnish.

Directions:

1. In a bowl or large resealable bag, combine the yogurt, olive oil, lemon juice and zest, garlic, honey, balsamic vinegar, oregano, thyme, bay leaf, salt, pepper, and red pepper flakes. Mix well.
2. Add the lamb pieces and marinate, refrigerated, for 30 minutes. Preheat the oven to 375°F. Thread the lamb onto the skewers, alternating with chunks of red onion as desired.
3. Put the skewers onto a baking sheet and roast for 10 to 15 minutes, rotating every 5 minutes to ensure that they cook evenly.
4. Plate the skewers and allow them to rest briefly. Top or serve with the yogurt dressing. To finish, garnish with fresh chopped parsley and a lemon wedge.

Nutrition:

- Calories: 578.
- Protein: 56 g.
- Fat: 30 g.
- Carbs: 20 g.

73. Garlic Pork Tenderloin and Lemony Orzo

Preparation Time: 15 minutes.
Cooking Time: 20 minutes.
Servings: 6
Ingredients:

- 1 pound pork tenderloin.
- ½ tsp. shawarma spice rub.
- 1 tbsp. salt.
- ½ tsp. coarsely ground black pepper.
- ½ tsp. garlic powder.
- 6 tbsp. extra-virgin olive oil.
- 3 cups lemony orzo.

Directions:

1. Preheat the oven to 350°F. Rub the pork with shawarma seasoning, salt, pepper, and garlic powder and drizzle with olive oil.
2. Put the pork on a baking sheet and roast for 20 minutes, or until the desired doneness. Remove the pork from the oven and let rest for 10 minutes. Assemble the pork on a plate with the orzo and enjoy.

Nutrition:

- Calories: 579.
- Protein: 33 g.
- Fat: 34 g.
- Carbs: 37 g.

74. Roasted Pork With Apple-Dijon Sauce

Preparation Time: 15 minutes.
Cooking Time: 40 minutes.
Servings: 8
Ingredients:

- 1 ½ tbsp. extra-virgin olive oil.
- 1 (12 oz.) pork tenderloin.
- ¼ tsp. kosher salt.
- ¼ tsp. freshly ground black pepper.
- ¼ cup apple jelly.
- ¼ cup apple juice.
- 2 to 3 tbsp. Dijon mustard.
- ½ tbsp. cornstarch.
- ½ tbsp. cream.

Directions:

1. Preheat the oven to 325°F. In a large sauté pan or skillet, heat the olive oil over medium heat.
2. Add the pork to the skillet, using tongs to turn and sear the pork on all sides. Once seared, sprinkle pork with salt and pepper, and set it on a small baking sheet.

3. In the same skillet, with the juices from the pork, mix the apple jelly, juice, and mustard into the pan juices. Heat thoroughly over low heat, stirring consistently for 5 minutes. Spoon over the pork.

4. Put the pork in the oven and roast for 15 to 17 minutes, or 20 minutes per pound. Every 10 to 15 minutes, baste the pork with the apple-mustard sauce.

5. Once the pork tenderloin is done, remove it from the oven and let it rest for 15 minutes. Then, cut it into 1-inch slices.

6. In a small pot, blend the cornstarch with cream. Heat over low heat. Add the pan juices into the pot, stirring for 2 minutes, until thickened. Serve the sauce over the pork.

Nutrition:
- Calories: 146.
- Protein: 13 g.
- Fat: 7 g.
- Carbs: 8 g.

75. Pressure Cooker Moroccan Pot Roast

Preparation Time: 15 minutes.
Cooking Time: 50 minutes.
Servings: 4
Ingredients:
- 8 oz. mushrooms, sliced.
- 4 tbsp. extra-virgin olive oil.
- 3 small onions, cut into 2-inch pieces.
- 2 tbsp. paprika.
- 1 ½ tbsp. garam masala.
- 2 tsp. salt.
- ¼ tsp. ground white pepper.
- 2 tbsp. tomato paste.
- 1 small eggplant, peeled and diced.
- 1 ¼ cups low-Sodium beef broth.
- ½ cup halved apricots.
- $^1/_3$ cup golden raisins.
- 3 pounds beef chuck roast.
- 2 tbsp. honey.
- 1 tbsp. dried mint.
- 2 cups cooked brown rice.

Directions:
1. Set an electric pressure cooker to Sauté and put the mushrooms and oil in the cooker. Sauté for 5 minutes, then add the onions, paprika, garam masala, salt, and white pepper. Stir in the tomato paste and continue to sauté.

2. Add the eggplant and sauté for 5 more minutes, until softened. Pour in the broth. Add the apricots and raisins. Sear the meat for 2 minutes on each side. Close and lock the lid and set the pressure cooker too high for 50 minutes.

3. When cooking is complete, quickly release the pressure. Carefully remove the lid, then remove the meat from the sauce and break it into pieces. While the meat is removed, stir honey and mint into the sauce.

4. Assemble plates with ½ cup of brown rice, ½ cup of pot roast sauce, and 3 to 5 pieces of pot roast.

Nutrition:
- Calories: 829
- Protein: 69 g.
- Fat: 34 g.
- Carbs: 70 g.

76. Shawarma Pork Tenderloin With Pitas

Preparation Time: 15 minutes.
Cooking Time: 35 minutes.
Servings: 8
Ingredients:
For the shawarma spice rub:
- 1 tsp. ground cumin.
- 1 tsp. ground coriander.
- 1 tsp. ground turmeric.
- ¾ tsp. sweet Spanish paprika.
- ½ tsp. ground cloves.
- ¼ tsp. salt.
- ¼ tsp. freshly ground black pepper.
- $^1/_8$ tsp. ground cinnamon.

For the shawarma:
- 1 ½ pound pork tenderloin.
- 3 tbsp. extra-virgin olive oil.
- 1 tbsp. garlic powder.
- Salt.
- Freshly ground black pepper.
- 1 ½ tbsp. shawarma spice rub.
- 4 pita pockets, halved, for serving.
- 1 to 2 tomatoes, sliced, for serving.
- ¼ cup pickled onions, for serving.
- ¼ cup pickled turnips, for serving.
- ¼ cup store-bought hummus or garlic-lemon hummus.

Directions:

To make the shawarma seasoning:

1. In a small bowl, combine the cumin, coriander, turmeric, paprika, cloves, salt, pepper, and cinnamon and set aside.

To make the shawarma:

1. Preheat the oven to 400°F. Put the pork tenderloin on a plate and cover it with olive oil and garlic powder on each side.
2. Season with salt and pepper and rub each side of the tenderloin with a generous amount of shawarma spices.
3. Place the pork tenderloin in the center of a roasting pan and roast for 20 minutes per pound, or until the meat begins to bounce back as you poke it.
4. If it feels like there's still fluid under the skin, continue cooking. Check every 5 to 7 minutes until it reaches the desired tenderness and juices run clear.
5. Remove the pork from the oven and let rest for 10 minutes. Serve the pork tenderloin shawarma with pita pockets, tomatoes, pickled onions (if using), pickled turnips (if using), and hummus.

Nutrition:

- Calories: 316.
- Protein: 29 g.
- Fat: 15 g.
- Carbs: 17 g.

77. Flank Steak With Artichokes

Preparation Time: 15 minutes.

Cooking Time: 60 minutes.

Servings: 4 to 6

Ingredients:

- 4 tbsp. grapeseed oil, divided.
- 2 pounds flank steak.
- 1 (14 oz.) can artichoke hearts, drained and roughly chopped.
- 1 onion, diced.
- 8 garlic cloves, chopped.
- 1 (32 oz.) container low-Sodium beef broth.
- 1 (14.5 oz.) can diced tomatoes, drained.
- 1 cup tomato sauce.
- 2 tbsp. tomato paste.
- 1 tsp. dried oregano.
- 1 tsp. dried parsley.
- 1 tsp. dried basil.
- ½ tsp. ground cumin.
- 3 bay leaves.

- 2 to 3 cups cooked couscous (optional).

Directions:

1. Preheat the oven to 450°F. In an oven-safe sauté pan or skillet, heat 3 tbsp. of oil on medium heat.
2. Sear the steak for 2 minutes per side on both sides. Transfer the steak to the oven for 30 minutes, or until desired tenderness.
3. Meanwhile, in a large pot, combine the remaining 1 tbsp. of oil, artichoke hearts, onion, and garlic.
4. Pour in the beef broth, tomatoes, tomato sauce, and tomato paste. Stir in oregano, parsley, basil, cumin, and bay leaves.
5. Cook the vegetables, covered, for 30 minutes. Remove bay leaf and serve with flank steak and ½ cup of couscous per plate, if using.

Nutrition:

- Calories: 577.
- Protein: 55 g.
- Fat: 28 g.
- Carbs: 22 g.

78. Easy Honey-Garlic Pork Chops

Preparation Time: 15 minutes.

Cooking Time: 25 minutes.

Servings: 4

Ingredients:

- 4 pork chops, boneless or bone-in.
- ¼ tsp. salt.
- $1/8$ tsp. freshly ground black pepper.
- 3 tbsp. extra-virgin olive oil.
- 5 tbsp. low-Sodium chicken broth, divided.
- 6 garlic cloves, minced.
- ¼ cup honey.
- 2 tbsp. apple cider vinegar.

Directions:

1. Season the pork chops with salt and pepper and set aside.
2. In a large sauté pan or skillet, heat the oil over medium-high heat. Add the pork chops and sear for 5 minutes on each side, or until golden brown.
3. Once the searing is complete, move the pork to a dish and reduce the skillet heat from medium-high to medium.
4. Add 3 tbsp. of chicken broth to the pan; this will loosen the bits and flavors from the bottom of the skillet.

5. Once the broth has evaporated, add the garlic to the skillet and cook for 15 to 20 seconds, until fragrant.

6. Add the honey, vinegar, and the remaining 2 tbsp. of broth. Bring the heat back up to medium-high and continue to cook for 3 to 4 minutes.

7. Stir periodically; the sauce is ready once it's thickened slightly. Add the pork chops back into the pan, cover them with the sauce, and cook for 2 minutes. Serve.

Nutrition:
- Calories: 302.
- Protein: 22 g.
- Fat: 16 g.
- Carbs: 19 g.

79. Sesame Beef

Preparation Time: 10 minutes.
Cooking Time: 15 minutes.
Servings: 4
Ingredients:
- 1-pound, grass-fed sirloin steak, sliced into thin strips.
- 4 tbsp. almond flour, divided.
- 1 cup peanut oil.

For the sauce:
- 1 green onion, thinly sliced.
- 1 tsp. minced garlic.
- 1 tbsp. grated ginger.
- ¼ cup brown Sugar.
- ¼ cup soy sauce.
- 2 tbsp. apple cider vinegar.
- 1 tbsp. Sriracha sauce.
- 2 tbsp. orange juice.
- 1 tsp. sesame oil.
- 1 tsp. sesame seeds.

Directions:
1. Place steak strips in a large bowl, add 2 tbsp. of almond flour and toss until coat.

2. Then sprinkle with the remaining 2 tbsp. of cornstarch.

3. Place a large skillet pan over medium heat, add peanut oil and when hot, add steak strips in a single layer and cook for 3 minutes until crispy.

4. Cook remaining steak strips in the same manner and then transfer to a plate lined with a paper towel.

5. Whisk together garlic, ginger, Sugar, soy sauce, vinegar, Sriracha sauce, orange juice, sesame oil and add to a medium saucepan.

6. Place this saucepan over medium-high heat and cook for 2 minutes or until slightly thick.

7. Add steak and stir until combined.

8. Garnish with sesame seeds and green onion and serve.

Nutrition:
- Calories: 412.3.
- Protein: 24.5 g.
- Fat: 31.3 g.
- Fiber: 3.8 g.
- Carbs: 8.8 g.

80. Moussaka

Preparation Time: 15 minutes.
Cooking Time: 40 minutes.
Servings: 6 to 8
Ingredients:
For the eggplant:
- 2 pounds eggplant, cut into ¼-inch-thick slices.
- 1 tsp. salt
- 2 to 3 tbsp. extra-virgin olive oil.

For the filling:
- 1 tbsp. extra-virgin olive oil.
- 2 shallots, diced.
- 1 tbsp. dried, minced garlic.
- 1 pound ground lamb.
- 4 oz. portobello mushrooms, diced.
- 1 (14.5 oz.) can crushed tomatoes, drained.
- ¼ cup tomato paste.
- 1 cup low-Sodium beef broth.
- 2 bay leaves.
- 2 tsp. dried oregano.
- ¾ tsp. salt.
- 2 ½ cups store-bought béchamel sauce.
- $^1/_3$ cup panko bread crumbs.

Directions:

To make the eggplant:

1. Preheat the oven to 450°F. Line large baking sheets with paper towels and arrange the eggplant slices in a single layer and sprinkle with salt.
2. Place another layer of paper towel on the eggplant slices. Continue until all eggplant slices are covered.
3. Let the eggplant sweat for 30 minutes to remove excess moisture. While this is happening, make the meat sauce.
4. Pat the eggplant dry. Dry the baking sheets and brush with oil and place the eggplant slices onto the baking sheets.
5. Bake for 15 to 20 minutes, or until lightly browned and softened. Remove from the oven and cool slightly before assembling the moussaka.

To make the filling:

1. In a large, oven-safe sauté pan or skillet, heat the olive oil over high heat. Cook the shallots and garlic for 2 minutes, until starting to soften.
2. Add the ground lamb and brown it with the garlic and onions, breaking it up as it cooks. Add the mushrooms and cook for 5 to 7 minutes, or until they have dehydrated slightly.
3. Add the tomatoes and paste, beef broth, bay leaves, oregano, and salt, and stir to combine.
4. Once the sauce is simmering, lower to medium-low and cook for 15 minutes, or until it reduces to a thick sauce. Remove the sauce to a separate bowl before assembly.
5. Reduce the oven temperature to 350°F. Place half the eggplant slices in the bottom of the skillet used to make the sauce. Top the slices with all the meat filling.
6. Place the remaining eggplant on top of the meat filling and pour the jarred béchamel sauce over the eggplant. Sprinkle with the bread crumbs.
7. Bake for 30 to 40 minutes or until golden brown. Let stand for 10 minutes before serving.

Nutrition:

- Calories: 491.
- Protein: 23 g.
- Fat: 33 g.
- Carbs: 30 g.

CHAPTER 12:

Poultry

81. Oven Roasted Garlic Chicken Thigh

Preparation Time: 10 minutes.
Cooking Time: 55 minutes.
Servings: 2
Ingredients:

- 8 chicken thighs.
- Salt and pepper as needed.
- 1 tbsp. extra-virgin olive oil.
- 6 garlic cloves, peeled and crushed.
- 1 jar (10 oz.) roasted red peppers, drained and chopped.
- 1 ½ pounds potatoes, diced.
- 2 cups cherry tomatoes, halved.
- $^1/_3$ cup capers, sliced.
- 1 tsp. dried Italian seasoning.
- 1 tbsp. fresh basil.

Directions:

1. Season chicken with kosher salt and black pepper.
2. Take a cast-iron skillet over medium-high heat and heat up olive oil.
3. Sear the chicken on both sides.
4. Add remaining Ingredients except for basil and stir well.
5. Remove heat and place cast iron skillet in the oven.
6. Bake for 45 minutes at 400°F until the internal temperature reaches 165°F.
7. Serve and enjoy!

Nutrition:

- Calories: 500.
- Protein: 35 g.
- Fat: 23 g.
- Carbs: 37 g.

82. Grilled Chicken Breasts

Preparation Time: 10 minutes.
Cooking Time: 15 minutes
Servings: 2
Ingredients:

- 4 boneless skinless chicken breasts.
- 3 tbsp. lemon juice.
- 3 tbsp. olive oil.
- 3 tbsp. chopped fresh parsley.
- 3 minced garlic cloves.
- 1 tsp. paprika.
- ½ tsp. dried oregano.
- Salt and pepper, to taste.

Directions:

1. In a large Ziploc bag, mix well oregano, paprika, garlic, parsley, olive oil, and lemon juice.
2. Pierce chicken with a knife several times and sprinkle with salt and pepper.
3. Add chicken to bag and marinate 20 minutes or up to 2 days in the fridge.
4. Remove chicken from bag and grill for 5 minutes per side in a 350°F preheated grill.
5. When cooked, transfer to a plate for 5 minutes before slicing.
6. Serve and enjoy with a side of rice or salad

Nutrition:

- Calories: 238.
- Protein: 24 g.
- Fats: 19 g.
- Carbs: 2 g.

83. Grilled Harass Chicken

Preparation Time: 20 minutes.
Cooking Time: 12 minutes.
Servings: 2
Ingredients:

- Juice 1 lemon.
- ½ sliced red onion.
- 1 ½ tsp. coriander.
- 1 ½ tsp. smoked paprika.
- 1 tsp. cumin.
- 2 tsp. cayenne.
- Olive oil.
- 1 ½ tsp. black pepper.
- Kosher salt.
- 5 oz. thawed and drained frozen spinach.
- 8 boneless chickens.

Directions:

1. Get a large bowl. Season your chicken with kosher salt on all sides, then add onions, garlic, lemon juice, and harass paste to the bowl.
2. Add about 3 tbsp. of olive oil to the mixture. Heat a grill to 459°F (an indoor or outdoor grill works just fine), then oil the grates.
3. Grill each side of the chicken for about 7 minutes. Its temperature should register 165°F on a thermometer and it should be fully cooked by then.

Nutrition:

- Calories: 142.5.
- Protein: 22.1 g.
- Fat: 4.7 g.
- Saturated Fat: 1.2 g.
- Sodium: 102 mg.
- Cholesterol: 107.4 mg.
- Carbs: 1.7 g.

84. Turkey Meatballs

Preparation Time: 10 minutes.
Cooking Time: 25 minutes.
Servings: 2
Ingredients:

- ¼ diced yellow onion.
- 14 oz. diced artichoke hearts.
- 1 pound ground turkey.
- 1 tsp. dried parsley.
- 1 tsp. oil.
- 4 tbsp. chopped basil.
- Pepper and salt, to taste.

Directions:

1. Grease the baking sheet and preheat the oven to 350°F.
2. On medium heat, place a nonstick medium saucepan, sauté artichoke hearts, and diced onions for 5 minutes or until onions are soft.
3. Meanwhile, in a big bowl, mix parsley, basil, and ground turkey with your hands. Season to taste.
4. Once the onion mixture has cooled, add it into the bowl and mix thoroughly.
5. With an ice cream scooper, scoop ground turkey and form balls.
6. Place on a prepared cooking sheet, pop in the oven, and bake until cooked around 15 to 20 minutes.
7. Remove from pan, serve and enjoy.

Nutrition:

- Calories: 283.
- Protein: 12 g.
- Fat: 12 g.
- Carbs: 30 g.

85. Chicken Marsala

Preparation Time: 10 minutes.
Cooking Time: 45 minutes.
Servings: 2
Ingredients:

- 2 tbsp. olive oil.
- 4 skinless, boneless chicken breast cutlets.
- ¾ tbsp. black pepper, divided.
- ½ tsp. kosher salt, divided.
- 8 oz. mushrooms, sliced.
- 4 thyme sprigs.
- 0.2 quarts unsalted chicken stock.
- 2 Quarts marsala wine.
- 11/2 Tbsp. olive oil.
- 1 Tbsp. fresh thyme, chopped.

Directions:

1. Heat oil in a pan and fry chicken for 4 to 5 minutes per side. Remove chicken from the pan and set it aside.
2. In the same pan add thyme, mushrooms, salt, and pepper; stir fry for 1 to 2 minutes.
3. Add marsala wine, chicken broth, and cooked chicken. Let simmer for 10 to 12 minutes on low heat.
4. Add to a serving dish.
5. Enjoy.

Nutrition:

- Calories: 206.
- Protein: 8 g.
- Fat: 17 g.
- Carbs: 3 g.

86.   Buttery Garlic Chicken

Preparation Time: 5 minutes.
Cooking Time: 40 minutes.
Servings: 2
Ingredients:

- 2 tbsp. ghee, melted.
- 2 boneless skinless chicken breasts.
- 1 Tbsp. dried Italian seasoning.
- 4 tbsp. butter.
- ¼ cup grated Parmesan cheese.
- A pinch of Himalayan salt, to taste.
- 1 tbsp Pepper, to taste.

Directions:

1. Preheat the oven to 375°F. Select a baking dish that fits both chicken breasts and coat it with ghee.
2. Pat dries the chicken breasts. Season with pink Himalayan salt, pepper, and Italian seasoning. Place the chicken in the baking dish.
3. In a medium skillet over medium heat, melt the butter. Sauté minced garlic, for about 5 minutes.
4. Remove the butter-garlic mixture from the heat, and pour it over the chicken breasts.
5. Roast in the oven for 30 to 35 minutes. Sprinkle some of the Parmesan cheese on top of each chicken breast. Let the chicken rest in the baking dish for 5 minutes.
6. Divide the chicken between two plates, spoon the butter sauce over the chicken, and serve.

Nutrition:

- Calories: 642.
- Protein: 57 g.
- Fat: 45 g.

87.   Creamy Chicken-Spinach Skillet

Preparation Time: 10 minutes.
Cooking Time: 17 minutes.
Servings: 2
Ingredients:

- 1 pound boneless skinless chicken breast.
- 1 medium diced onion.
- 12 oz. diced roasted red peppers.
- 2 ½ cups. chicken stock.
- 2 cups baby spinach leaves.
- 2 cups cooked pasta.
- 2 tbsp. butter.
- 4 minced garlic cloves.
- 7 oz. cream cheese,
- A pinch of Salt and pepper, to taste.

Directions:

1. Place a saucepan on medium-high heat for 2 minutes. Add butter and melt for a minute, swirling to coat the pan.
2. Add chicken to a pan, season with pepper and salt to taste. Cook chicken on high heat for 3 minutes per side.
3. Lower heat to medium and stir in onions, red peppers, and garlic. Sauté for 5 minutes and deglaze the pot with a little bit of stock.
4. Whisk in chicken stock and cream cheese. Cook and mix until thoroughly combined.
5. Stir in spinach and adjust seasoning to taste. Cook for 2 minutes or until spinach is wilted.
6. Serve and enjoy.

Nutrition:

- Calories: 484.
- Protein: 36 g.
- Fats: 22 g.
- Carbs: 33 g.

88.   Creamy Chicken Breasts

Preparation Time: 10 minutes.
Cooking Time: 12 minutes.
Servings: 4
Ingredients:

- 4 chicken breasts, skinless and boneless.
- 1 tbsp. basil pesto.
- 1 ½ tbsp. cornstarch.
- ¼ cup roasted red peppers, chopped.
- $1/_3$ cup heavy cream.
- 1 tsp. Italian seasoning,
- 1 tsp. garlic, minced.
- 1 cup chicken broth.
- ½ tbsp Pepper.
- A pinch of Salt.

Directions:

1. Add chicken into the instant pot. Season chicken with Italian seasoning, pepper, and salt. Sprinkle with garlic. Pour broth over chicken. Seal pot with lid and cook on high for 8 minutes.
2. Once done, allow to release pressure naturally for 5 minutes then release remaining using quick release. Remove lid. Transfer chicken to a plate and clean the instant pot.
3. Set the instant pot on sauté mode. Add heavy cream, pesto, cornstarch, and red pepper to the pot and stir well and cook for 3 to 4 minutes.

4. Return chicken to the pot and coat well with the sauce. Serve and enjoy.

Nutrition:
- Calories: 341. Protein: 43.8 g.
- Fat: 15.2 g. Carbs: 4.4 g.

89. Cheese Garlic Chicken & Potatoes

Preparation Time: 10 minutes.
Cooking Time: 13 minutes.
Servings: 4
Ingredients:
- 2 pounds chicken breasts, skinless, boneless, cut into chunks. - 1 tbsp. olive oil.
- ¾ cup chicken broth. - 1 tbsp. Italian seasoning.
- 1 tbsp. garlic powder. - 1 tsp. garlic, minced.
- 1 ½ cup parmesan cheese, shredded.
- 1 pound potatoes, chopped.
- Pepper.
- Salt.

Directions:
1. Add oil into the inner pot of the instant pot and set the pot on sauté mode. Add chicken and cook until browned. Add remaining ingredients except for cheese and stir well.
2. Seal the pot with the lid and cook on high for 8 minutes. Once done, release pressure using quick release. Remove the lid. Top with cheese and cover with lid for 5 minutes or until cheese is melted. Serve and enjoy.

Nutrition:
- Calories: 674. Protein: 79.7 g.
- Fat: 29 g. Carbs: 21.4 g.

90. Easy Chicken Scampi

Preparation Time: 10 minutes.
Cooking Time: 25 minutes.
Servings: 4
Ingredients:
- 3 chicken breasts, skinless, boneless, and sliced.

- 1 tsp. garlic, minced.
- 1 tbsp. Italian seasoning.
- 2 cups chicken broth.
- 1 bell pepper, sliced.
- ½ onion, sliced.
- Pepper.
- Salt.

Directions:
1. Add chicken into the instant pot and top with remaining Ingredients. Seal pot with lid and cook on high for 25 minutes. Once done, release pressure using quick release. Remove lid.
2. Remove chicken from pot and shred using a fork. Return shredded chicken to the pot and stir well. Serve over cooked whole grain pasta and top with cheese.

Nutrition:
- Calories: 254. Protein: 34.6 g.
- Fat: 9.9 g. Carbs: 4.6 g.

91. Protein-Packed Chicken Bean Rice

Preparation Time: 10 minutes.
Cooking Time: 15 minutes.
Servings: 6
Ingredients:
- 1 pound chicken breasts, skinless, boneless, and cut into chunks.
- 14 oz. can cannellini beans, rinsed and drained.
- 4 cups chicken broth.
- 2 cups brown rice.
- 1 tbsp. Italian seasoning.
- 1 small onion, chopped.
- 1 tbsp. garlic, chopped.
- 1 tbsp. olive oil.
- Pepper.
- Salt.

Directions:
1. Add oil into the inner pot of the instant pot and set the pot on sauté mode. Add garlic and onion and sauté for 3 minutes. Add remaining Ingredients and stir everything well.
2. Seal pot with a lid and select manual and set timer for 12 minutes. Once done, release pressure using quick release. Remove lid. Stir well and serve.

Nutrition:
- Calories: 494. Protein: 34.2 g.
- Fat: 11.3 g. Carbs: 61.4 g.

92. Pesto Vegetable Chicken

Preparation Time: 10 minutes.

Cooking Time: 25 minutes.

Servings: 4

Ingredients:

- 1 ½ pound chicken thighs, skinless, boneless, and cut into pieces.
- ½ cup chicken broth.
- ¼ cup fresh parsley, chopped.
- 2 cups cherry tomatoes, halved.
- 1 cup basil pesto.
- ¾ pound asparagus, trimmed and cut in half.
- $^2/_3$ cup sun-dried tomatoes, drained and chopped.
- 2 tbsp. olive oil.
- Pepper.
- Salt.

Directions:

1. Add oil into the inner pot of the instant pot and set the pot on sauté mode. Add chicken and sauté for 5 minutes. Add remaining Ingredients except for tomatoes and stir well.
2. Seal pot with a lid and select manual and set timer for 15 minutes. Once done, release pressure using quick release. Remove lid.
3. Add tomatoes and stir well. Again, seal the pot and select manual, and set the timer for 5 minutes. Release pressure using quick release. Remove lid. Stir well and serve.

Nutrition:

- Calories: 459.
- Protein: 9.2 g.
- Fat: 20.5 g.
- Carbs: 14.9 g.

93. Greek Chicken Rice

Preparation Time: 10 minutes.

Cooking Time: 14 minutes.

Servings: 4

Ingredients:

- 3 chicken breasts, skinless, boneless, and cut into chunks.
- ¼ fresh parsley, chopped.
- 1 zucchini, sliced.
- 2 bell peppers, chopped.
- 1 cup rice, rinsed and drained.
- 1 ½ cup chicken broth.
- 1 tbsp. oregano.
- 3 tbsp. fresh lemon juice.
- 1 tbsp. garlic, minced.

- 1 onion, diced.
- 2 tbsp. olive oil.
- Pepper.
- Salt.

Directions:

1. Add oil into the inner pot of the instant pot and set the pot on sauté mode. Add onion and chicken and cook for 5 minutes. Add rice, oregano, lemon juice, garlic, broth, pepper, and salt, and stir everything well.
2. Seal pot with lid and cook on high for 4 minutes. Once done, release pressure using quick release. Remove lid. Add parsley, zucchini, and bell peppers and stir well.
3. Seal pot again with lid and select manual and set timer for 5 minutes. Release pressure using quick release. Remove lid. Stir well and serve.

Nutrition:

- Calories: 500.
- Protein: 38.7 g.
- Fat: 16.5 g.
- Carbs: 48 g.

94. Flavorful Chicken Tacos

Preparation Time: 10 minutes.

Cooking Time: 10 minutes.

Servings: 3

Ingredients:

- 2 chicken breasts, skinless and boneless.
- 1 tbsp. chili powder.
- ½ tsp. ground cumin.
- ½ tsp. garlic powder.
- ¼ tsp. onion powder.
- ½ tsp. paprika.
- 4 oz. can green chilis, diced.
- ¼ cup chicken broth.
- 14 oz. can tomato, diced.
- Pepper.
- Salt.

Directions:

1. Add all Ingredients except chicken into the instant pot and stir well. Add chicken and stir. Seal pot with lid and cook on high for 10 minutes.
2. Once done, allow to release pressure naturally for 5 minutes then release remaining using quick release. Remove lid.
3. Remove chicken from pot and shred using a fork.

4. Return shredded chicken to the pot and stir well. Serve and enjoy.

Nutrition:

- Calories: 237.
- Protein: 30.5 g.
- Fat: 8 g.
- Carbs: 10.8 g.

95. Quinoa Chicken Bowls

Preparation Time: 10 minutes.

Cooking Time: 6 minutes.

Servings: 4

Ingredients:

- 1 pound chicken breasts, skinless, boneless, and cut into chunks.
- 14 oz. can chickpeas, drained and rinsed.
- 1 cup olives, pitted and sliced.
- 1 cup cherry tomatoes, halved.
- 1 cucumber, sliced.
- 2 tsp. Greek seasoning.
- 1 ½ cups chicken broth.
- 1 cup quinoa, rinsed and drained.
- Pepper.
- Salt.

Directions:

1. Add broth and quinoa into the instant pot and stir well. Season chicken with Greek seasoning, pepper, and salt and place it into the instant pot.
2. Seal pot with lid and cook on high for 6 minutes. Once done, release pressure using quick release. Remove lid. Stir quinoa and chicken mixture well.
3. Add remaining Ingredients and stir everything well. Serve immediately and enjoy it.

Nutrition:

- Calories: 566.
- Protein: 46.8 g.
- Fat: 16.4 g.
- Carbs: 57.4 g.

96. Quick Chicken With Mushrooms

Preparation Time: 10 minutes.

Cooking Time: 22 minutes.

Servings: 6

Ingredients:

- 2-pound chicken breasts, skinless and boneless. - ½ cup heavy cream.
- $^{1}/_{3}$ cup water. - ¾ pounds mushrooms, sliced.
- 3 tbsp. olive oil.
- 1 tsp. Italian seasoning. - Pepper.
- Salt.

Directions:

1. Add oil into the inner pot of the instant pot and set the pot on sauté mode. Season chicken with Italian seasoning, pepper, and salt.
2. Add chicken to the pot and sauté for 5 minutes. Remove chicken from pot and set aside. Add mushrooms and sauté for 5 minutes or until mushrooms are lightly brown.
3. Return chicken to the pot. Add water and stir well. Seal pot with a lid and select manual and set timer for 12 minutes.
4. Once done, release pressure using quick release. Remove lid. Remove chicken from pot and place on a plate.
5. Set pot on sauté mode. Add heavy cream and stir well and cook for 5 minutes. Pour mushroom sauce over chicken and serve.

Nutrition:

- Calories: 396. Protein: 45.7 g.
- Fat: 22.3 g. Carbs: 2.2 g.

97. Herb Garlic Chicken

Preparation Time: 10 minutes.

Cooking Time: 12 minutes.

Servings: 8

Ingredients:

- 4 pounds chicken breasts, skinless and boneless.

- 1 tbsp. garlic powder.
- 2 tbsp. dried Italian herb mix.
- 2 tbsp. olive oil.
- ¼ cup chicken stock.
- Pepper.
- Salt.

Directions:

1. Coat chicken with oil and season with dried herb, garlic powder, pepper, and salt. Place chicken into the instant pot. Pour stock over the chicken. Seal pot with a lid and select manual and set timer for 12 minutes.
2. Once done, allow to release pressure naturally for 5 minutes then release remaining using quick release. Remove lid. Shred chicken using a fork and serve.

Nutrition:

- Calories: 502. Protein: 66.8 g.
- Fat: 20.8 g. Carbs: 7.8 g.

98. Flavorful Mediterranean Chicken

Preparation Time: 10 minutes.
Cooking Time: 20 minutes.
Servings: 8
Ingredients:

- 2 pounds chicken thighs.
- ½ cup olives.
- 28 oz. can tomato, diced.
- 1 ½ tsp. dried oregano.
- 2 tsp. dried parsley.
- ½ tsp. ground coriander powder.
- ¼ tsp. chili pepper.
- 1 tsp. onion powder.
- 1 tsp. paprika.
- 2 cups onion, chopped.
- 2 tbsp. olive oil.
- Pepper.
- Salt.

Directions:

1. Add oil into the inner pot of the instant pot and set the pot on sauté mode. Add chicken and cook until browned. Transfer chicken on a plate. Add onion and sauté for 5 minutes.
2. Add all spices, tomatoes, and salt and cook for 2 to 3 minutes. Return chicken to the pot and stir everything well. Seal pot with lid and cook on high for 8 minutes.
3. Once done, release pressure using quick release. Remove lid. Add olives and stir well. Serve and enjoy.

Nutrition:

- Calories: 292. Protein: 34.3 g.
- Fat: 13 g. Carbs: 8.9 g.

99. Artichoke Olive Chicken

Preparation Time: 10 minutes.
Cooking Time: 8 minutes.
Servings: 6
Ingredients:

- 2 ½ pounds chicken breasts, skinless and boneless.
- 14 oz. can artichokes.
- ½ cup olives, pitted.
- ¾ cup prunes.
- 1 tbsp. capers.
- 1 ½ tbsp. garlic, chopped.
- 3 tbsp. red wine vinegar.
- 2 tsp. dried oregano.
- $^1/_3$ cup wine.
- Pepper.
- Salt.

Directions:

1. Add all Ingredients except chicken into the instant pot and stir well. Add chicken and mix well. Seal pot with lid and cook on high for 8 minutes.
2. Once done, allow to release pressure naturally for 10 minutes then release remaining using quick release. Remove lid. Serve and enjoy.

Nutrition:

- Calories: 472. Protein: 57.6 g.
- Fat: 15.5 g. Carbs: 22.7 g.

100. Easy Chicken Piccata

Preparation Time: 10 minutes.
Cooking Time: 41 minutes.
Servings: 6
Ingredients:

- 8 chicken thighs, bone-in, and skin-on.
- 2 tbsp. fresh parsley, chopped.

- 1 tbsp. olive oil.
- 3 tbsp. capers.
- 2 tbsp. fresh lemon juice.
- ½ cup chicken broth.
- ¼ cup dry white wine.
- 1 tbsp. garlic, minced.

Directions:

1. Add oil into the inner pot of the instant pot and set the pot on sauté mode. Add garlic and sauté for 1 minute. Add wine and cook for 5 minutes or until wine is reduced by half.
2. Add lemon juice and broth and stir well. Add chicken and seal pot with the lid and select manual and set a timer for 30 minutes.
3. Once done, release pressure using quick release. Remove lid. Remove chicken from pot and place on a baking tray. Broil chicken for 5 minutes. Add capers and stir well. Garnish with parsley and serve.

Nutrition:

- Calories: 406.
- Protein: 57 g.
- Fat: 17 g.
- Carbs: 1.2 g.

101. Garlic Thyme Chicken Drumsticks

Preparation Time: 10 minutes.
Cooking Time: 18 minutes.
Servings: 4
Ingredients:

- 8 chicken drumsticks, skin-on.
- 2 tbsp. balsamic vinegar.
- 2/3 cup can tomato, diced.
- 6 garlic cloves.
- 1 tsp. lemon zest, grated.
- 1 tsp. dried thyme.
- ¼ tsp. red pepper flakes.
- 1 ½ onion, cut into wedges.
- 1 tbsp. olive oil.
- Pepper.
- Salt.

Directions:

1. Add oil into the inner pot of the instant pot and set the pot on sauté mode. Add onion and ½ tsp. of salt and sauté for 2 to 3 minutes.
2. Add chicken, garlic, lemon zest, red pepper flakes, and thyme and mix well. Add vinegar and tomatoes and stir well.

3. Seal pot with lid and cook on high for 15 minutes. Once done, release pressure using quick release. Remove lid. Stir well and serve.

Nutrition:

- Calories: 220.
- Protein: 26.4 g.
- Fat: 8.9 g.
- Carbs: 7.8 g.

102. Tender Chicken & Mushrooms

Preparation Time: 10 minutes.
Cooking Time: 21 minutes.
Servings: 6
Ingredients:

- 1 pound chicken breasts, skinless, boneless, & cut into 1-inch pieces.
- ¼ cup olives, sliced.
- 2 oz. feta cheese, crumbled.
- ¼ cup sherry.
- 1 cup chicken broth.
- 1 tsp. Italian seasoning.
- 12 oz. mushrooms, sliced.
- 2 celery stalks, diced.
- 1 tsp. garlic, minced.
- ½ cup onion, chopped.
- 2 tbsp. olive oil.
- Pepper. - Salt.

Directions:

1. Add oil into the inner pot of the instant pot and set the pot on sauté mode. Add mushrooms, celery, garlic, and onion, and sauté for 5 to 7 minutes.
2. Add chicken, Italian seasoning, pepper, and salt and stir well and cook for 4 minutes. Add sherry and broth and stir well. Seal pot with lid and cook on high for 10 minutes.
3. Once done, allow to release pressure naturally for 10 minutes then release remaining using quick release. Remove lid. Add olives and feta cheese and stir well. Serve and enjoy.

Nutrition:

- Calories: 244. Protein: 26 g.
- Fat: 13.5 g. Carbs: 4.1 g.

103. Delicious Chicken Casserole

Preparation Time: 10 minutes.
Cooking Time: 20 minutes.
Servings: 4
Ingredients:

- 1 pound chicken breasts, skinless, boneless, & cubed.

- 2 tsp. paprika.
- 3 tbsp. tomato paste.
- 1 cup chicken stock.
- 4 tomatoes, chopped.
- 1 small eggplant, chopped.
- 1 tbsp. Italian seasoning.
- 2 bell peppers, sliced.
- 1 onion, sliced.
- 1 tbsp. garlic, minced.
- 1 tbsp. olive oil.
- Pepper.
- Salt.

Directions:

1. Add oil into the inner pot of the instant pot and set the pot on sauté mode. Season chicken with pepper and salt and add into the instant pot. Cook chicken until lightly golden brown.
2. Remove chicken from pot and place on a plate. Add garlic and onion and sauté until onion is softened about 3 to 5 minutes.
3. Return chicken to the pot. Pour remaining Ingredients over the chicken and stir well. Seal pot with lid and cook on high for 10 minutes.
4. Once done, release pressure using quick release. Remove lid. Stir well and serve.

Nutrition:

- Calories: 356.
- Protein: 36.9 g.
- Fat: 13.9 g.
- Carbs: 22.7 g.

104. Perfect Chicken & Rice

Preparation Time: 10 minutes.
Cooking Time: 25 minutes.
Servings: 4
Ingredients:

- 1 pound chicken breasts, skinless and boneless.
- 1 tsp. olive oil.
- 1 cup onion, diced.
- 1 tsp. garlic minced.
- 4 carrots, peeled and sliced.
- 1 tbsp. Mediterranean spice mix.
- 2 cups brown rice, rinsed.
- 2 cups chicken stock.
- Pepper.
- Salt.

Directions:

1. Add oil into the inner pot of the instant pot and set the pot on sauté mode. Add garlic and onion and sauté until onion is softened.
2. Add stock, carrot, rice, and Mediterranean spice mix and stir well. Place chicken on top of the rice mixture and season with pepper and salt. Do not mix.
3. Seal pot with a lid and select manual and set timer for 20 minutes. Once done, allow to release pressure naturally for 10 minutes then release remaining using quick release. Remove lid.
4. Remove chicken from pot and shred using a fork. Return shredded chicken to the pot and stir well. Serve and enjoy.

Nutrition:

- Calories: 612.
- Protein: 41.1 g.
- Fat: 12.4 g.
- Carbs: 81.7 g.

105. Moroccan Chicken

Preparation Time: 10 minutes.
Cooking Time: 25 minutes.
Servings: 6
Ingredients:

- 2 pounds chicken breasts, cut into chunks.
- ½ tsp. cinnamon.
- 1 tsp. turmeric.
- ½ tsp. ginger.
- 1 tsp. cumin.
- 2 tbsp. Dijon mustard.
- 1 tbsp. molasses.
- 1 tbsp. honey.
- 2 tbsp. tomato paste.
- 5 garlic cloves, chopped.
- 2 onions, cut into quarters.
- 2 green bell peppers, cut into strips.
- 2 red bell peppers, cut into strips.
- 2 cups olives, pitted.
- 1 lemon, peeled and sliced.
- 2 tbsp. olive oil.
- Pepper.
- Salt.

Directions:

1. Add oil into the inner pot of the instant pot and set the pot on sauté mode. Add chicken and sauté for 5 minutes. Add remaining Ingredients and stir everything well.
2. Seal pot with a lid and select manual and set timer for 20 minutes. Once done, release pressure using quick release.

3. Remove lid. Stir well and serve.

Nutrition:
- Calories: 446.
- Protein: 45.8 g.
- Fat: 21.2 g.
- Carbs: 18.5 g.

106. Flavorful Cafe Rio Chicken

Preparation Time: 10 minutes.
Cooking Time: 12 minutes.
Servings: 6
Ingredients:
- 2 pounds chicken breasts, skinless and boneless.
- ½ cup chicken stock.
- 2 ½ tbsp. ranch seasoning.
- ½ tbsp. ground cumin.
- ½ tbsp. chili powder.
- ½ tbsp. garlic, minced.
- ²/₃ cup Italian dressing.
- Pepper.
- Salt.

Directions:
1. Add chicken into the instant pot. Mix together remaining Ingredients and pour over chicken. Seal pot with a lid and select manual and set timer for 12 minutes.
2. Once done, allow to release pressure naturally for 10 minutes then release remaining using quick release. Remove lid. Shred the chicken using a fork and serve.

Nutrition:
- Calories: 382. Protein: 44.1 g.
- Fat: 18.9 g.
- Carbs: 3.6 g.

107. Zesty Veggie Chicken

Preparation Time: 10 minutes.
Cooking Time: 5 minutes.
Servings: 4
Ingredients:
- 1 pound chicken tender, skinless, boneless and cut into chunks.
- 10 oz. frozen vegetables.
- ¹/₃ cup zesty Italian dressing.
- ½ tsp. Italian seasoning.
- 1 cup fried onions.
- ²/₃ cup rice.
- 1 cup chicken broth.
- Pepper.
- Salt.

Directions:
1. Add all Ingredients except vegetables into the instant pot. Meanwhile, cook frozen vegetables in the microwave according to packet instructions.
2. Seal pot with lid and cook on high for 5 minutes. Once done, allow to release pressure naturally for 10 minutes then release remaining using quick release. Remove lid.
3. Add cooked vegetables and stir well. Serve and enjoy.

Nutrition:
- Calories: 482.
- Protein: 38.3 g.
- Fat: 15.9 g.
- Carbs: 40.5 g.

108. Chicken From Milan

Preparation Time: 10 minutes.
Cooking Time: 30 minutes.
Servings: 4
Ingredients:
- 1 tbsp. butter.
- Salt and pepper to taste.
- 2 garlic cloves, minced.
- 2 tbsp. vegetable oil.
- ½ cup sun-dried tomatoes, diced.
- 2 tbsp. diced fresh basil.
- 1 cup chicken broth, divided.
- 8 oz. dry fettuccini pasta.
- 1 cup heavy cream.
- 1 pound skinless, boneless chicken breast halves.

Directions:
1. Coat a cookie sheet with oil then set your oven to 350°F before doing anything else.
2. Stir fry your garlic for 1 min in butter, then combine in ¾ cups of broth and the tomatoes.
3. Turn up the heat and get everything boiling.

4. Once the mix is boiling, set the heat to low, and let the contents cook for 12 minutes.
5. Now add in the cream and get everything boiling again until the mix is thick.
6. Coat your chicken all over with pepper and salt then fry the meat in hot oil for 5 minutes on each side until fully done. Then place the chicken to the side in a covered bowl.
7. Remove some of the drippings from the pan and begin to get ¼ cup of broth boiling while scraping the bottom bits.
8. Once the mix is boiling, set the heat to low, add in the basil, and let the broth reduce a bit.
9. Once it has been reduced, combine it with the tomato cream sauce.
10. Now begin to boil your pasta in water and salt for 9 minutes then remove the liquid and place everything in a bowl. Stir the pasta with about 5 tbsp. of tomato cream sauce.
11. Now slice your chicken into strips and get the tomato hot again. Divide your noodles between serving dishes. Top the noodles with some chicken and then some sauce. Enjoy.

Nutrition:
- Calories: 641.
- Protein: 36.3 g.
- Fat: 34.8 g.
- Cholesterol: 156 mg.
- Sodium: 501 mg.
- Carbs: 47 g.

109. Traditional Chicken Shawarma

Preparation Time: 15 minutes.
Cooking Time: 15 minutes.
Servings: 4 to 6
Ingredients:
- 2 pounds (907 g.) boneless and skinless chicken.
- ½ cup lemon juice.
- ½ cup extra-virgin olive oil.
- 3 tbsp. minced garlic.
- 1 ½ tsp. salt.
- ½ tsp. freshly ground black pepper.
- ½ tsp. ground cardamom.
- ½ tsp. cinnamon.
- Hummus and pita bread, for serving (optional).

Directions:
1. Cut the chicken into ¼-inch strips and put them into a large bowl.
2. In a separate bowl, whisk together the lemon juice, olive oil, garlic, salt, pepper, cardamom, and cinnamon.
3. Pour the dressing over the chicken and stir to coat all of the chicken.
4. Let the chicken sit for about 10 minutes.
5. Heat a large pan over medium-high heat and cook the chicken pieces for 12 minutes, using tongs to turn the chicken over every few minutes.
6. Serve with hummus and pita bread, if desired.

Nutrition:
- Calories: 477.
- Protein: 47 g.
- Fat: 32 g.
- Fiber: 1 g.
- Sodium: 1234 mg.
- Carbs: 5 g.

110. Chicken Shish Tawook

Preparation Time: 15 minutes.
Cooking Time: 15 minutes.
Servings: 4 to 6
Ingredients:
- 2 tbsp. garlic, minced.
- 2 tbsp. tomato paste.
- 1 tsp. smoked paprika.
- ½ cup lemon juice.
- ½ cup extra-virgin olive oil.
- 1 ½ tsp. salt.
- ½ tsp. freshly ground black pepper.
- 2 pounds (907 g.) boneless and skinless chicken (breasts or thighs).
- Rice, tzatziki, or hummus, for serving (optional).

Directions:
1. In a large bowl, add the garlic, tomato paste, paprika, lemon juice, olive oil, salt, and pepper and whisk to combine.
2. Cut the chicken into ½-inch cubes and put them into the bowl; toss to coat with the marinade. Set aside for at least 10 minutes.
3. To grill, preheat the grill on high. Thread the chicken onto skewers and cook for 3 minutes per side, for a Total of 9 minutes.
4. To cook in a pan, preheat the pan on high heat, add the chicken, and cook for 9 minutes, turning over the chicken using tongs.

5. Serve the chicken with rice, tzatziki, or hummus, if desired.

Nutrition:

- Calories: 482.
- Fat: 32 g.
- Protein: 47 g.
- Fiber: 1 g.
- Sodium: 1298 mg.
- Carbs: 6 g.

111. Lemon-Garlic Whole Chicken and Potatoes

Preparation Time: 10 minutes.
Cooking Time: 45 minutes.
Servings: 4 to 6
Ingredients:

- 1 cup garlic, minced.
- 1 ½ cups lemon juice.
- 1 cup + 2 tbsp. extra-virgin olive oil, divided.
- 1 ½ tsp. salt, divided.
- 1 tsp. freshly ground black pepper.
- 1 whole chicken, cut into 8 pieces.
- 1 pound (454 g.) fingerling or red potatoes.

Directions:

1. Preheat the oven to 400ºF (205ºC).
2. In a large bowl, whisk together the garlic, lemon juice, 1 cup of olive oil, 1 tsp. of salt, and pepper.
3. Put the chicken in a large baking dish and pour half of the lemon sauce over the chicken. Cover the baking dish with foil, and cook for 20 minutes.
4. Cut the potatoes in half, and toss to coat with 2 tbsp. of olive oil and 1 tsp. of salt. Put them on a baking sheet and bake for 20 minutes in the same oven as the chicken.
5. Take both the chicken and potatoes out of the oven. Using a spatula, transfer the potatoes to the baking dish with the chicken. Pour the remaining sauce over the potatoes and chicken. Bake for another 25 minutes.
6. Transfer the chicken and potatoes to a serving dish and spoon the garlic-lemon sauce from the pan on top.

Nutrition:

- Calories: 959.
- Fat: 78 g.
- Protein: 33 g.
- Fiber: 4 g.
- Sodium: 1005 mg.
- Carbs: 37 g.

112. Lemon Chicken Thighs With Vegetables

Preparation Time: 15 minutes.
Cooking Time: 45 minutes.
Servings: 4
Ingredients:

- 6 tbsp. extra-virgin olive oil, divided.
- 4 large garlic cloves, crushed.
- 1 tbsp. dried basil.
- 1 tbsp. dried parsley.
- 1 tbsp. salt.
- ½ tbsp. thyme.
- 4 skin-on, bone-in chicken thighs.
- 6 medium portobello mushrooms, quartered.
- 1 large zucchini, sliced.
- 1 large carrot, thinly sliced.
- ⅛ cup pitted Klamath olives.
- 8 pieces sun-dried tomatoes (optional.)
- ½ cup dry white wine.
- 1 lemon, sliced.

Directions:

1. In a small bowl, combine 4 tbsp. of olive oil, garlic cloves, basil, parsley, salt, and thyme. Store half of the marinade in a jar and, in a bowl, combine the remaining half to marinate the chicken thighs for about 30 minutes.
2. Preheat the oven to 425°F (220°C).
3. In a large skillet or oven-safe pan, heat the remaining 2 tbsp. of olive oil over medium-high heat. Sear the chicken for 3 to 5 minutes on each side until golden brown, and set aside.
4. In the same pan, sauté portobello mushrooms, zucchini, and carrot for about 5 minutes, or until lightly browned.
5. Add the chicken thighs, olives, and sun-dried tomatoes (if using). Pour the wine over the chicken thighs.
6. Cover the pan and cook for about 10 minutes over medium-low heat.
7. Uncover the pan and transfer it to the oven. Cook for 15 more minutes, or until the chicken skin is crispy and the juices run clear. Top with lemon slices.

Nutrition:

- Calories: 544.
- Protein: 28 g.
- Fat: 41 g.
- Fiber: 11 g.
- Sodium: 1848 mg.
- Carbs: 20 g.

113. Feta Stuffed Chicken Breasts

Preparation Time: 10 minutes.
Cooking Time: 20 minutes.
Servings: 4
Ingredients:

- ⅓ cup cooked brown rice.
- 1 tsp. shawarma seasoning.
- 4 (6 oz./170 g.) boneless skinless chicken breasts.
- 1 tbsp. harass.
- 3 tbsp. extra-virgin olive oil, divided.
- Salt and freshly ground black pepper, to taste.
- 4 small dried apricots, halved.
- ⅓ cup crumbled feta.
- 1 tbsp. chopped fresh parsley.

Directions:

1. Preheat the oven to 375°F (190°C).
2. In a medium bowl, mix the rice and shawarma seasoning and set aside.
3. Butterfly the chicken breasts by slicing them almost in half, starting at the thickest part and folding them open like a book.
4. In a small bowl, mix the harass with 1 tbsp. of olive oil. Brush the chicken with the harass oil and season with salt and pepper. The harass adds a nice heat, so feel free to add a thicker coating for more spice.
5. Onto one side of each chicken breast, spoon 1 to 2 tbsp. of rice, then layer 2 apricot halves in each breast. Divide the feta between the chicken breasts and fold the other side over the filling to close.
6. In an oven-safe sauté pan or skillet, heat the remaining 2 tbsp. of olive oil and sear the breast for 2 minutes on each side, then place the pan into the oven for 15 minutes, or until fully cooked and juices run clear. Serve, garnished with parsley.

Nutrition:

- Calories: 321. Fat: 17 g.
- Protein: 37 g. Fiber: 1 g.
- Sodium: 410 mg.
- Carbs: 8 g.

114. Greek Lemon Chicken Kebabs

Preparation Time: 15 minutes.
Cooking Time: 20 minutes.
Servings: 2
Ingredients:

- ½ cup extra-virgin olive oil, divided.
- ½ large lemon, juiced.
- 2 garlic cloves, minced.
- ½ tsp. za'atar seasoning.
- Salt and freshly ground black pepper, to taste.
- 1 pound (454 g) boneless skinless chicken breasts, cut into 1¼-inch cubes.
- 1 large red bell pepper, cut into 1¼-inch pieces.
- 2 small zucchini (nearly 1 pound/454 g), cut into rounds slightly under ½ inch thick.
- 2 large shallots, diced into quarters.
- Tzatziki sauce, for serving.

Directions:

1. In a bowl, whisk together ⅓ cup of olive oil, lemon juice, garlic, za'atar, salt, and pepper. Put the chicken in a medium bowl and pour the olive oil mixture over the chicken. Press the chicken into the marinade. Cover and refrigerate for 45 minutes. While the chicken marinates, soak the wooden skewers in water for 30 minutes.
2. Drizzle and toss the pepper, zucchini, and shallots with the remaining 2 ½ tbsp. of olive oil and season lightly with salt.
3. Preheat the oven to 500°F (260°C) and put a baking sheet in the oven to heat.
4. On each skewer, thread a red bell pepper, zucchini, shallot, and 2 chicken pieces and repeat twice. Put the kebabs onto the hot baking sheet and cook for 7 to 9 minutes, or until the chicken is cooked through. Rotate once halfway through cooking. Serve the kebabs warm with the tzatziki sauce.

Nutrition: (2 kebabs)

- Calories: 825.
- Protein: 51 g.
- Fat: 59 g.
- Fiber: 5 g.
- Sodium: 379 mg.
- Carbs: 31 g.

115. Moroccan Chicken Meatballs

Preparation Time: 10 minutes.
Cooking Time: 10 minutes.
Servings: 4 to 6
Ingredients:

- 2 large shallots, diced.
- 2 tbsp. finely chopped parsley.
- 2 tsp. paprika.
- 1 tsp. ground cumin.
- ½ tsp. ground coriander.
- ½ tsp. garlic powder.
- ½ tsp. salt.
- ½ tsp. freshly ground black pepper.
- ⅛ tsp. ground cardamom.
- 1 pound (454 g.) ground chicken.
- ½ cup all-purpose flour, to coat.
- ¼ cup olive oil, divided.

Directions:

1. In a bowl, combine the shallots, parsley, paprika, cumin, coriander, garlic powder, salt, pepper, and cardamom. Mix well.
2. Add the chicken to the spice mixture and mix well. Form into 1-inch balls flattened to about ½-inch thickness.
3. Put the flour in a bowl for dredging. Dip the balls into the flour until coated.
4. Pour enough oil to cover the bottom of a sauté pan or skillet and heat over medium heat. Working in batches, cook the meatballs, turning frequently, for 2 to 3 minutes on each side, until they are cooked through. Add more oil between batches as needed. Serve in a pita, topped with lettuce dressed with creamy yogurt dressing.

Nutrition:

- Calories: 405.
- Protein: 24 g.
- Fat: 26 g.
- Fiber: 1 g.
- Sodium: 387 mg.
- Carbs: 20 g.

116. Spatchcock Chicken With Lemon and Rosemary

Preparation Time: 20 minutes.
Cooking Time: 45 minutes.
Servings: 6 to 8
Ingredients:

- ½ cup extra-virgin olive oil, divided.
- 1 (3- to 4-pound /1.4- to 1.8-kg) roasting chicken.
- 8 garlic cloves, roughly chopped.
- 2 to 4 tbsp. chopped fresh rosemary.
- 2 tsp. salt, divided.
- 1 tsp. freshly ground black pepper, divided.
- 2 lemons, thinly sliced.

Directions:

1. Preheat the oven to 425°F (220°C).
2. Pour 2 tbsp. of olive oil in the bottom of a 9-by-13-inch baking dish or rimmed baking sheet and swirl to coat the bottom.
3. To spatchcock the bird, place the whole chicken breast-side down on a large work surface. Using a very sharp knife, cut along the backbone, starting at the tail end and working your way up to the neck. Pull apart the two sides, opening up the chicken. Flip it over, breast-side up, pressing down with your hands to flatten the bird. Transfer to the prepared baking dish.
4. Loosen the skin over the breasts and thighs by cutting a small incision and sticking 1 or 2 fingers inside to pull the skin away from the meat without removing it.
5. To prepare the filling, in a small bowl, combine ¼ cup olive oil, garlic, rosemary, 1 tsp. of salt, and ½ tsp. of pepper and whisk together.
6. Rub the garlic-herb oil evenly under the skin of each breast and each thigh. Add the lemon slices evenly to the same areas.
7. Whisk together the remaining 2 tbsp. of olive oil, 1 tsp. of salt, and ½ tsp. of pepper and rub over the outside of the chicken.
8. Place in the oven, uncovered, and roast for 45 minutes, or until cooked through and golden brown. Allow resting 5 minutes before carving to serve.

Nutrition:

- Calories: 435.
- Protein: 28 g.
- Fat: 34 g.
- Fiber: 0 g.
- Sodium: 879 mg.
- Carbs: 2 g.

117. Chicken Skewers With Veggies

Preparation Time: 30 minutes.
Cooking Time: 25 minutes.
Servings: 4
Ingredients:

- ¼ cup olive oil.
- 1 tsp. garlic powder.

- 1 tsp. onion powder.
- 1 tsp. ground cumin.
- ½ tsp. dried oregano.
- ½ tsp. dried basil.
- ¼ cup lemon juice.
- 1 tbsp. apple cider vinegar.
- Olive oil cooking spray.
- 1 pound (454 g.) boneless skinless chicken thighs, cut into 1-inch pieces.
- 1 red bell pepper, cut into 1-inch pieces.
- 1 red onion, cut into 1-inch pieces.
- 1 zucchini, cut into 1-inch pieces.
- 12 cherry tomatoes.

Directions:

1. In a large bowl, mix together the olive oil, garlic powder, onion powder, cumin, oregano, basil, lemon juice, and apple cider vinegar.
2. Spray six skewers with olive oil cooking spray.
3. On each skewer, slide on a piece of chicken, then a piece of bell pepper, onion, zucchini, and finally a tomato, and then repeat. Each skewer should have at least two pieces of each item.
4. Once all of the skewers are prepared, place them in a 9-by-13-inch baking dish and pour the olive oil marinade over the top of the skewers. Turn each skewer so that all sides of the chicken and vegetables are coated.
5. Cover the dish with plastic wrap and place it in the refrigerator for 30 minutes.
6. After 30 minutes, preheat the air fryer to 380°F (193°C). (If using a grill attachment, make sure it is inside the air fryer during preheating.)
7. Remove the skewers from the marinade and lay them in a single layer in the air fryer basket. If the air fryer has a grill attachment, you can also lay them on this instead.
8. Cook for 10 minutes. Rotate the kebabs, then cook them for 15 minutes more.
9. Remove the skewers from the air fryer and let them rest for 5 minutes before serving.

Nutrition:

- Calories: 304.
- Fat: 17 g.
- Protein: 27 g.
- Carbs: 10 g.
- Fiber: 3 g.
- Sodium: 62 mg.

118. Yogurt-Marinated Chicken

Preparation Time: 15 minutes.
Cooking Time: 30 minutes.
Servings: 2
Ingredients:

- ½ cup plain Greek yogurt.
- 3 garlic cloves, minced.
- 2 tbsp. minced fresh oregano (or 1 tbsp. dried oregano).
- Zest 1 lemon.
- 1 tbsp. olive oil.
- ½ tsp. salt.
- 2 (4 oz./ 113-g.) boneless, skinless chicken breasts.

Directions:

1. In a medium bowl, add the yogurt, garlic, oregano, lemon zest, olive oil, and salt and stir to combine. If the yogurt is very thick, you may need to add a few tbsp. of water or a squeeze of lemon juice to thin it a bit.
2. Add the chicken to the bowl and toss it in the marinade to coat it well. Cover and refrigerate the chicken for at least 30 minutes or up to overnight.
3. Preheat the oven to 350°F (180°C) and set the rack to the middle position.
4. Place the chicken in a baking dish and roast for 30 minutes, or until the chicken reaches an internal temperature of 165°F (74°C).

Nutrition:

- Calories: 255.
- Protein: 29 g.
- Fat: 13 g.
- Fiber: 2 g.
- Sodium: 694 mg.
- Carbs: 8 g.

119. Chicken, Mushrooms, and Tarragon Pasta

Preparation Time: 15 minutes.
Cooking Time: 15 minutes.
Servings: 2
Ingredients:

- 2 tbsp. olive oil, divided.
- ½ medium onion, minced.
- 4 oz. (113 g.) baby Bella (cremini) mushrooms, sliced.
- 2 small garlic cloves, minced.
- 8 oz. (227 g.) chicken cutlets.
- 2 tsp. tomato paste.
- 2 tsp. dried tarragon.
- 2 cups low-Sodium chicken stock.
- 6 oz. (170 g.) pappardelle pasta.
- ¼ cup plain full-Fat Greek yogurt.
- Salt, to taste.
- Freshly ground black pepper, to taste.

Directions:

1. Heat 1 tbsp. of the olive oil in a sauté pan over medium-high heat. Add the onion and mushrooms and sauté for 5 minutes. Add the garlic and cook for 1 minute more.
2. Move the vegetables to the edges of the pan and add the remaining 1 tbsp. of olive oil to the center of the pan. Place the cutlets in the center and let them cook for about 3 minutes, or until they lift up easily and are golden brown on the bottom.
3. Flip the chicken and cook for another 3 minutes.
4. Mix in the tomato paste and tarragon. Add the chicken stock and stir well to combine everything. Bring the stock to a boil.
5. Add the pappardelle. Break up the pasta if needed to fit into the pan. Stir the noodles so they don't stick to the bottom of the pan.
6. Cover the sauté pan and reduce the heat to medium-low. Let the chicken and noodles simmer for 15 minutes, stirring occasionally until the pasta is cooked and the liquid is mostly absorbed. If the liquid absorbs too quickly and the pasta isn't cooked, add more water or chicken stock, about ¼ cup at a time as needed.
7. Remove the pan from the heat.
8. Stir 2 tbsp. of the hot liquid from the pan into the yogurt. Pour the tempered yogurt into the pan and stir well to mix it into the sauce. Season with salt and pepper.
9. The sauce will tighten up as it cools, so if it seems too thick, add a few tbsp. of water.

Nutrition:

- Calories: 556.
- Protein: 42 g.
- Fat: 17 g.
- Fiber: 1 g.
- Sodium: 190 mg.
- Carbs: 56 g.

120. Chicken Sausage and Tomato With Farro

Preparation Time: 10 minutes.
Cooking Time: 45 minutes.
Servings: 2
Ingredients:

- 1 tbsp. olive oil
- ½ medium onion, diced.
- ¼ cup julienned sun-dried tomatoes packed in olive oil and herbs.
- 8 oz. (227 g) hot Italian chicken sausage, removed from the casing.
- ¾ cup farro.
- 1 ½ cups low-Sodium chicken stock.
- 2 cups loosely packed arugula.
- 4 to 5 large fresh basil leaves, sliced thin.
- Salt, to taste.

Directions:

1. Heat the olive oil in a sauté pan over medium-high heat. Add the onion and sauté for 5 minutes. Add the sun-dried tomatoes and chicken sausage, stirring to break up the sausage. Cook for 7 minutes, or until the sausage is no longer pink.
2. Stir in the farro. Let it toast for 3 minutes, stirring occasionally.
3. Add the chicken stock and bring the mixture to a boil. Cover the pan and reduce the heat to medium-low. Let it simmer for 30 minutes, or until the farro is tender.
4. Stir in the arugula and let it wilt slightly. Add the basil, and season with salt.

Nutrition:

- Calories: 491.
- Protein: 31 g.
- Fat: 18 g.
- Fiber: 6 g.
- Sodium: 765 mg.
- Carbs: 53 g.

CHAPTER 13:

Fish and Seafood Recipes

121. Shrimp With Garlic and Mushrooms

Preparation Time: 15 minutes.

Cooking Time: 15 minutes.

Servings: 4

Ingredients:

- 1 pound (454 g.) peeled and deveined fresh shrimp.
- 1 tsp. salt.
- 1 cup extra-virgin olive oil.
- 8 large garlic cloves, thinly sliced.
- 4 oz. (113 g.) sliced mushrooms (shiitake, baby Bella, or button).
- ½ tsp. red pepper flakes.
- ¼ cup chopped fresh flat-leaf Italian parsley.
- Zucchini noodles or riced cauliflower, for serving.

Directions:

1. Rinse the shrimp and pat dry. Place in a small bowl and sprinkle with salt. In a large rimmed, thick skillet, heat the olive oil over medium-low heat.
2. Add the garlic and heat until very fragrant, 3 to 4 minutes, reducing the heat if the garlic starts to burn.
3. Add the mushrooms and sauté for 5 minutes, until softened. Add the shrimp and red pepper flakes and sauté until the shrimp begins to turn pink for another 3 to 4 minutes.

4. Remove from the heat and stir in the parsley. Serve over zucchini noodles or riced cauliflower.

Nutrition:

- Calories: 620.
- Protein: 24 g.
- Fat: 56 g.
- Carbs: 4 g.

122. Pistachio-Crusted Whitefish

Preparation Time: 10 minutes.

Cooking Time: 20 minutes.

Servings: 2

Ingredients:

- ¼ cup shelled pistachios.
- 1 tbsp. fresh parsley.
- 1 tbsp. grated Parmesan cheese.
- 1 tbsp. panko bread crumbs.
- 2 tbsp. olive oil.
- ¼ tsp. salt.
- 10 oz. skinless whitefish (1 large piece or 2 smaller ones).

Directions:

1. Preheat the oven to 350°F and set the rack to the middle position. Line a sheet pan with foil or parchment paper.
2. Combine all of the Ingredients except the fish in a mini food processor, and pulse until the nuts are finely ground.
3. Alternatively, you can mince the nuts with a chef's knife and combine the Ingredients by hand in a small bowl.
4. Place the fish on the sheet pan. Spread the nut mixture evenly over the fish and pat it down lightly.
5. Bake the fish for 20 to 30 minutes, depending on the thickness, until it flakes easily with a fork.
6. Keep in mind that a thicker cut of fish takes a bit longer to bake. You'll know it's done when it's opaque, flakes apart easily with a fork, or reaches an internal temperature of 145°F

Nutrition:

- Calories: 185.
- Protein: 10.1 g.
- Fat: 5.2 g.
- Carbs: 23.8 g.

123. Seafood Risotto

Preparation Time: 15 minutes.

Cooking Time: 30 minutes.

Servings: 4

Ingredients:

- 6 cups vegetable broth.
- 3 tbsp. extra-virgin olive oil.
- 1 large onion, chopped.
- 3 garlic cloves, minced.
- ½ tsp. saffron threads.
- 1 ½ cups arborio rice.
- 1 ½ tsp. salt.
- 8 oz. (227 g.) shrimp (21 to 25), peeled and deveined.
- 8 oz. (227 g.) scallops.

Directions:

1. In a large saucepan over medium heat, bring the broth to a low simmer. In a large skillet over medium heat, cook the olive oil, onion, garlic, and saffron for 3 minutes.
2. Add the rice, salt, and 1 cup of broth to the skillet. Stir the Ingredients together and cook over low heat until most of the liquid is absorbed.
3. Repeat steps with broth, adding ½ cup of broth at a time, and cook until all but ½ cup of the broth is absorbed.
4. Add the shrimp and scallops when you stir in the final ½ cup of broth. Cover and let cook for 10 minutes. Serve warm.

Nutrition:

- Calories: 460. Protein: 24 g.
- Fat: 12 g. Carbs: 64 g.

124. Crispy Homemade Fish Sticks Recipe

Preparation Time: 10 minutes.

Cooking Time: 15 minutes.

Servings: 2

Ingredients:

- ½ cup flour.
- 1 beaten egg.
- 1 cup of flour.
- ½ cup parmesan cheese.
- ½ cup bread crumbs.
- Zest1 lemon juice.
- Parsley.
- Salt.
- 1 tsp. black pepper
- 1 tbsp. sweet paprika.
- 1 tsp. oregano.
- 1 ½ pound salmon.
- Extra virgin olive oil.

Directions:

1. Preheat your oven to about 450°F. Get a bowl, dry your salmon, and season its two sides with salt.
2. Then chop into small sizes of 1½ inch length each. Get a bowl and mix black pepper with oregano.
3. Add paprika to the mixture and blend it. Then spice the fish stick with the mixture you have just made. Get another dish and pour your flours.
4. You will need a different bowl again to pour your egg wash into. Pick yet the fourth dish, mix your breadcrumb with your parmesan and add lemon zest to the mixture.
5. Return to the fish sticks and dip each fish into flour such that both sides are coated with flour. As you dip each fish into flour, take it out and dip it into the egg wash and lastly, dip it in the breadcrumb mixture.
6. Do this for all fish sticks and arrange them on a baking sheet. Ensure you oil the baking sheet before arranging the stick thereon and drizzle the top of the fish sticks with extra virgin olive oil.
7. **Caution:** allow excess flours to fall off a fish before dipping it into other Ingredients. Also, ensure that you do not let the coating peel while you add extra virgin olive oil on top of the fish. Fix the baking sheet in the middle of the oven and allow it to cook for 13 min. By then, the fishes should be golden brown and you can collect them from the oven, and you can serve them immediately.
8. Top it with your lemon zest, parsley, and fresh lemon juice.

Nutrition:

- Calories: 119 Protein: 13.5 g.
- Fat: 3.4 g. Sodium: 293.1 mg. Carbs: 9.3 g.

125. Sauced Shellfish in White Wine

Preparation Time: 10 minutes.

Cooking Time: 10 minutes.

Servings: 2

Ingredients:

- 2 pounds fresh cuttlefish.
- ½ cup olive oil.
- 1 pc large onion, finely chopped.
- 1 cup robola white wine.
- ¼ cup lukewarm water.
- 1 pc bay leaf.
- ½ bunch parsley, chopped.
- 4 pcs tomatoes, grated.
- Salt and pepper.

Directions:

1. Take out the hard centerpiece of cartilage (cuttlebone), the bag of ink, and the intestines from the cuttlefish.
2. Wash the cleaned cuttlefish with running water. Slice it into small pieces, and drain excess water.
3. Heat the oil in a saucepan placed over medium-high heat and sauté the onion for 3 minutes until tender.
4. Add the sliced cuttlefish and pour in the white wine. Cook for 5 minutes until it simmers.
5. Pour in the water, and add the tomatoes, bay leaf, parsley, salt, and pepper. Simmer the mixture over low heat until the cuttlefish slices are tender and left with their thick sauce. Serve them warm with rice.
6. Be careful not to overcook the cuttlefish as its texture becomes very hard. A safe rule of thumb is grilling the cuttlefish over a ragingly hot fire for 3 minutes before using it in any recipe.

Nutrition:

- Calories: 308. Protein: 25.6 g.
- Fats: 18.1 g.
- Dietary Fiber: 1.5 g.
- Carbs: 8 g.

126. Garlic Shrimp Black Bean Pasta

Preparation Time: 15 minutes.

Cooking Time: 15 minutes.

Servings: 4

Ingredients:

- 1 pound (454 g.) black bean linguine or spaghetti.
- 1 pound (454 g.) fresh shrimp, peeled and deveined.
- 4 tbsp. extra-virgin olive oil.
- 1 onion, finely chopped.
- 3 garlic cloves, minced.
- ¼ cup basil, cut into strips.

Directions:

1. Bring a large pot of water to a boil and cook the pasta according to the package instructions.
2. In the last 5 minutes of cooking the pasta, add the shrimp to the hot water and allow them to cook for 3 to 5 minutes.
3. Once they turn pink, take them out of the hot water, and, if you think you may have overcooked them, run them under cool water. Set aside.
4. Reserve 1 cup of the pasta cooking water and drain the noodles. In the same pan, heat the oil over medium-high heat and cook the onion and garlic for 7 to 10 minutes.
5. Once the onion is translucent, add the pasta back in and toss well. Plate the pasta, then top with shrimp and garnish with basil.

Nutrition:

- Calories: 668.
- Protein: 57 g.
- Fat: 19 g.
- Carbs: 73 g.

127. Pistachio Sole Fish

Preparation Time: 5 minutes.

Cooking Time: 10 minutes.

Servings: 2

Ingredients:

- 4 (5 oz.) boneless sole fillets.
- ½ cup pistachios, finely chopped.
- 1 lemon Juice.
- 1 Tsp. extra virgin olive oil.
- A pinch Salt and pepper, to taste.

Directions:

1. Preheat your oven to 350°F.
2. Wrap baking sheet using parchment paper and keep it on the side
3. Pat fish dry with kitchen towels and lightly season with salt and pepper
4. Take a small bowl and stir in pistachios
5. Place sol on the prepped sheet and press 2 tbsp. of pistachio mixture on top of each fillet
6. Rub the fish with lemon juice and olive oil

7. Bake for 10 minutes until the top is golden and fish flakes with a fork

Nutrition:

- Calories: 166.
- Fat: 6 g.
- Carbs: 2 g.

128. Speedy Tilapia With Red Onion and Avocado

Preparation Time: 10 minutes.
Cooking Time: 5 minutes.
Servings: 2
Ingredients:

- 1 tbsp. extra-virgin olive oil.
- 1 tbsp. freshly squeezed orange juice.
- ¼ tsp. kosher or sea salt.
- 4 (4 oz.) tilapia fillets, more oblong than square, skin-on, or skinned.
- ¼ cup chopped red onion (about $1/_8$ onion).
- 1 avocado, pitted, skinned, and sliced.

Directions:

1. In a 9-inch glass pie dish, use a fork to mix together the oil, orange juice, and salt. Working with one fillet at a time, place each in the pie dish and turn to coat on all sides.
2. Arrange the fillets in a wagon-wheel formation, so that one end of each fillet is in the center of the dish and the other end is temporarily draped over the edge of the dish.
3. Top each fillet with 1 tbsp. of onion, then fold the end of the fillet that's hanging over the edge in half over the onion.
4. When finished, you should have 4 folded-over fillets with the fold against the outer edge of the dish and the ends all in the center.
5. Cover the dish with plastic wrap, leaving a small part open at the edge to vent the steam. Microwave on high for about 3 minutes.
6. The fish is done when it just begins to separate into flakes (chunks) when pressed gently with a fork. Top the fillets with the avocado and serve.

Nutrition:

- Fiber: 3 g.
- Protein: 22 g.
- Carbs: 4 g.

129. Steamed Mussels in White Wine Sauce

Preparation Time: 5 minutes.
Cooking Time: 10 minutes.
Servings: 2
Ingredients:

- 2 pounds small mussels.
- 1 tbsp. extra-virgin olive oil.
- 1 cup thinly sliced red onion.
- 3 garlic cloves, sliced.
- 1 cup dry white wine.
- 2 (¼-inch-thick) lemon slices.
- ¼ tsp. freshly ground black pepper.
- ¼ tsp. kosher or sea salt.
- Fresh lemon wedges, for serving (optional).

Directions:

1. In a large colander in the sink, run cold water over the mussels (but don't let the mussels sit in standing water).
2. All the shells should be closed tight; discard any shells that are a little bit open or any shells that are cracked. Leave the mussels in the colander until you're ready to use them.
3. In a large skillet over medium-high heat, heat the oil. Add the onion and cook for 4 minutes, stirring occasionally.
4. Add the garlic and cook for 1 minute, stirring constantly. Add the wine, lemon slices, pepper, and salt, and bring to a simmer. Cook for 2 minutes.
5. Add the mussels and cover. Cook for 3 minutes, or until the mussels open their shells. Gently shake the pan two or three times while they are cooking.
6. All the shells should now be wide open. Using a slotted spoon, discard any mussels that are still closed. Spoon the opened mussels into a shallow serving bowl, and pour the broth over the top. Serve with additional fresh lemon slices, if desired.

Nutrition:

- Calories: 22, 7 g.
- Total Fat: 1 g.
- Fiber: 18 g.

130. Orange and Garlic Shrimp

Preparation Time: 20 minutes.

Cooking Time: 10 minutes.

Servings: 2

Ingredients:

- 1 large orange.
- 3 tbsp. extra-virgin olive oil, divided.
- 1 tbsp. chopped fresh rosemary.
- 1 tbsp. chopped fresh thyme.
- 3 garlic cloves, minced (about 1½ tsp.)
- ¼ tsp. freshly ground black pepper.
- ¼ tsp. kosher or sea salt.
- 1 ½ pound fresh raw shrimp, shells, and tails removed.

Directions:

1. Zest the entire orange using a citrus grater. In a large zip-top plastic bag, combine the orange zest and 2 tbsp. of oil with the rosemary, thyme, garlic, pepper, and salt.
2. Add the shrimp, seal the bag, and gently massage the shrimp until all the Ingredients are combined and the shrimp is completely covered with the seasonings. Set aside.
3. Heat a grill, grill pan, or a large skillet over medium heat. Brush on or swirl in the remaining 1 tbsp. of oil.
4. Add half the shrimp, and cook for 4 to 6 minutes, or until the shrimp turn pink and white, flipping halfway through if on the grill or stirring every minute if in a pan. Transfer the shrimp to a large serving bowl.
5. Repeat with the remaining shrimp, and add them to the bowl.
6. While the shrimp cook, peel the orange and cut the flesh into bite-size pieces. Add to the serving bowl, and toss with the cooked shrimp. Serve immediately or refrigerate and serve cold.

Nutrition:

- Calories: 190, 8 g.
- Total Fat: 1 g.
- Fiber: 24 g.

131. Roasted Shrimp-Gnocchi Bake

Preparation Time: 10 minutes.

Cooking Time: 20 minutes.

Servings: 2

Ingredients:

- 1 cup chopped fresh tomato.
- 2 tbsp. extra-virgin olive oil.
- 2 garlic cloves, minced.
- ½ tsp. freshly ground black pepper.
- ¼ tsp. crushed red pepper.
- 1 (12 oz.) jar roasted red peppers.
- 1 pound fresh raw shrimp, shells, and tails removed.
- 1 pound frozen gnocchi (not thawed).
- ½ cup cubed feta cheese.
- $1/_3$ cup fresh tore basil leaves.

Directions:

1. Preheat the oven to 425°F. In a baking dish, mix the tomatoes, oil, garlic, black pepper, and crushed red pepper. Roast in the oven for 10 minutes.
2. Stir in the roasted peppers and shrimp. Roast for 10 more minutes, until the shrimp turn pink and white.
3. While the shrimp cooks, cook the gnocchi on the stovetop according to the package Directions.
4. Drain in a colander and keep warm. Remove the dish from the oven. Mix in the cooked gnocchi, feta, and basil, and serve.

Nutrition:

- Calories: 227, 7 g.
- Total Fat: 1 g.
- Fiber: 20 g.

132. Spicy Shrimp Puttanesca

Preparation Time: 5 minutes.

Cooking Time: 15 minutes.

Servings: 2

Ingredients:

- 2 tbsp. extra-virgin olive oil.
- 3 anchovy fillets, drained and chopped.
- 3 garlic cloves, minced.
- ½ tsp. crushed red pepper.
- 1 (14.5 oz.) can low-Sodium or no-salt-added diced tomatoes, undrained.

- 1 (2.25 oz.) can sliced black olives, drained.
- 2 tbsp. capers.
- 1 tbsp. chopped fresh oregano.
- 1 pound fresh raw shrimp, shells, and tails removed.

Directions:

1. In a large skillet over medium heat, heat the oil. Mix in the anchovies, garlic, and crushed red pepper.
2. Cook for 3 minutes, stirring frequently and mashing up the anchovies with a wooden spoon until they have melted into the oil.
3. Stir in the tomatoes with their juices, olives, capers, and oregano. Turn up the heat to medium-high, and bring to a simmer.
4. When the sauce is lightly bubbling, stir in the shrimp. Reduce the heat to medium, and cook the shrimp for 6 to 8 minutes, or until they turn pink and white, stirring occasionally, and serve.

Nutrition:

- Calories: 214.
- Total Fat: 10 g.
- Fiber: 2 g.
- Protein: 26 g.

133. Baked Cod With Vegetables

Preparation Time: 15 minutes.
Cooking Time: 25 minutes.
Servings: 2
Ingredients:

- 1 pound (454 g.) thick cod fillet, cut into 4 even portions.
- ¼ tsp. onion powder (optional).
- ¼ tsp. paprika.
- 3 tbsp. extra-virgin olive oil.
- 4 medium scallions.
- ½ cup fresh chopped basil, divided.
- 3 tbsp. minced garlic (optional).

- 2 tsp. salt.
- 2 tsp. freshly ground black pepper.
- ¼ tsp. dry marjoram (optional).
- 6 sun-dried tomato slices.
- ½ cup dry white wine.
- ½ cup crumbled feta cheese.
- 1 (15 oz./ 425-g.) can oil-packed artichoke hearts, drained.
- 1 lemon, sliced.
- 1 cup pitted kalamata olives.
- 1 tsp. capers (optional).
- 4 small red potatoes, quartered.

Directions:

1. Set oven to 375°F (190°C).
2. Season the fish with paprika and onion powder (if desired).
3. Heat an ovenproof skillet over medium heat and sear the top side of the cod for about 1 minute until golden. Set aside.
4. Heat the olive oil in the same skillet over medium heat. Add the scallions, ¼ cup of basil, garlic (if desired), salt, pepper, marjoram (if desired), tomato slices, and white wine, and stir to combine. Boil then removes from heat.
5. Evenly spread the sauce on the bottom of the skillet. Place the cod on top of the tomato basil sauce and scatter with feta cheese. Place the artichokes in the skillet and top with the lemon slices.
6. Scatter with the olives, capers (if desired), and the remaining ¼ cup of basil. Pull out from the heat and transfer to the preheated oven. Bake for 15 to 20 minutes
7. Meanwhile, place the quartered potatoes on a baking sheet or wrapped in aluminum foil. Bake in the oven for 15 minutes.
8. Cool for 5 minutes before serving.

Nutrition:

- Calories: 1168.
- Fat: 60 g.
- Protein: 64 g.

134. Slow Cooker Salmon in Foil

Preparation Time: 5 minutes.
Cooking Time: 2 hours.
Servings: 2
Ingredients:

- 2 (6 oz./ 170-g.) salmon fillets.
- 1 tbsp. olive oil.
- 2 garlic cloves, minced.
- ½ tbsp. lime juice.

- 1 tsp. finely chopped fresh parsley.
- ¼ tsp. black pepper.

Directions:

1. Spread a length of foil onto a work surface and place the salmon fillets in the middle.
2. Blend olive oil, garlic, lime juice, parsley, and black pepper. Brush the mixture over the fillets. Fold the foil over and crimp the sides to make a packet.
3. Place the packet into the slow cooker, cover, and cook on High for 2 hours
4. Serve hot.

Nutrition:

- Calories: 446. Fat: 21 g.
- Protein: 65 g.

135. Dill Chutney Salmon

Preparation Time: 5 minutes.
Cooking Time: 3 minutes.
Servings: 2
Ingredients:
Chutney:

- ¼ cup fresh dill.
- ¼ cup extra virgin olive oil.
- Juice from ½ lemon.
- Sea salt, to taste.

Fish:

- 2 cups water.
- 2 salmon fillets.
- Juice from ½ lemon.
- ¼ tsp. paprika.
- Salt and freshly ground pepper to taste.

Directions:

1. Put all the chutney Ingredients in a food processor until creamy. Set aside.
2. Add the water and steamer basket to the Instant Pot. Place salmon fillets, skin-side down, on the steamer basket. Drizzle the lemon juice over salmon and sprinkle with the paprika.
3. Secure the lid. Select the Manual mode and set the Cooking Time for 3 minutes at High Pressure.
4. Once cooking is complete, do a quick pressure release. Carefully open the lid.
5. Season the fillets with pepper and salt to taste. Serve topped with the dill chutney.

Nutrition:

- Calories: 636.
- Fat: 41 g.
- Protein: 65 g.

136. Garlic-Butter Parmesan Salmon and Asparagus

Preparation Time: 10 minutes.
Cooking Time: 15 minutes.
Servings: 2
Ingredients:

- 2 (6 oz./ 170-g.) salmon fillets, skin on and patted dry.
- Pink Himalayan salt.
- Freshly ground black pepper, to taste.
- 1 pound (454 g.) fresh asparagus, ends snapped off.
- 3 tbsp. almond butter.
- 2 garlic cloves, minced.
- ¼ cup grated Parmesan cheese.

Directions:

1. Prep oven to 400°F (205°C). Line a baking sheet with aluminum foil.
2. Season both sides of the salmon fillets.
3. Situate salmon in the middle of the baking sheet and arrange the asparagus around the salmon.
4. Heat the almond butter in a small saucepan over medium heat.
5. Cook minced garlic
6. Drizzle the garlic-butter sauce over the salmon and asparagus and scatter the Parmesan cheese on top.
7. Bake in the preheated oven for about 12 minutes. You can switch the oven to broil at the end of Cooking Time for about 3 minutes to get a nice char on the asparagus.
8. Let cool for 5 minutes before serving.

Nutrition:

- Calories: 435.
- Fat: 26 g.
- Protein: 42 g.

137. Lemon Rosemary Roasted Branzino

Preparation Time: 15 minutes.
Cooking Time: 30 minutes.
Servings: 2
Ingredients:

- 4 tbsp. extra-virgin olive oil, divided.
- 2 (8 oz.) branzino fillets.
- 1 garlic clove, minced.
- 1 bunch scallions.
- 10 to 12 small cherry tomatoes, halved.
- 1 large carrot, cut into ¼-inch rounds.
- ½ cup dry white wine.

- 2 tbsp. paprika.
- 2 tsp. kosher salt.
- ½ tbsp. ground chili pepper.
- 2 rosemary sprigs or 1 tbsp. dried rosemary.
- 1 small lemon, thinly sliced.
- ½ cup sliced pitted kalamata olives.

Directions:

1. Heat a large ovenproof skillet over high heat until hot, about 2 minutes. Add 1 tbsp. of olive oil and heat
2. Add the branzino fillets, skin-side up, and sear for 2 minutes. Flip the fillets and cook. Set aside.
3. Swirl 2 tbsp. of olive oil around the skillet to coat evenly.
4. Add the garlic, scallions, tomatoes, and carrot, and sauté for 5 minutes
5. Add the wine, stirring until all Ingredients are well combined. Carefully place the fish over the sauce.
6. Preheat the oven to 450°F (235°C).
7. Brush the fillets with the remaining 1 tbsp. of olive oil and season with paprika, salt, and chili pepper. Top each fillet with a rosemary sprig and lemon slices. Scatter the olives over fish and around the skillet.
8. Roast for about 10 minutes until the lemon slices are browned. Serve hot.

Nutrition:

- Calories: 724.
- Fat: 43 g.
- Protein: 57 g.

138. Grilled Lemon Pesto Salmon

Preparation Time: 5 minutes.
Cooking Time: 10 minutes.
Servings: 2
Ingredients:

- 10 oz. (283 g) salmon fillet.

- 2 tbsp. prepared pesto sauce.
- 1 large fresh lemon, sliced.
- Cooking spray.

Directions:

1. Preheat the grill to medium-high heat. Spray the grill grates with cooking spray.
2. Season the salmon well. Spread the pesto sauce on top.
3. Make a bed of fresh lemon slices about the same size as the salmon fillet on the hot grill, and place the salmon on top of the lemon slices. Put any additional lemon slices on top of the salmon.
4. Grill the salmon for 10 minutes.
5. Serve hot.

Nutrition:

- Calories: 316.
- Protein: 29 g.
- Fat: 21 g.

139. Steamed Trout With Lemon Herb Crust

Preparation Time: 10 minutes.
Cooking Time: 15 minutes.
Servings: 2
Ingredients:

- 3 tbsp. olive oil.
- 3 garlic cloves, chopped.
- 2 tbsp. fresh lemon juice.
- 1 tbsp. chopped fresh mint.
- 1 tbsp. chopped fresh parsley.
- ¼ tsp. dried ground thyme.
- 1 tsp. sea salt.
- 1 pound (454 g.) fresh trout (2 pieces).
- 2 cups fish stock.

Directions:

1. Blend olive oil, garlic, lemon juice, mint, parsley, thyme, and salt. Brush the marinade onto the fish.
2. Insert a trivet in the Instant Pot. Fill in the fish stock and place the fish on the trivet.
3. Secure the lid. Select the Steam mode and set the Cooking Time for 15 minutes at High Pressure.
4. Once cooking is complete, do a quick pressure release. Carefully open the lid. Serve warm.

Nutrition:

- Calories: 477.
- Protein: 52 g.
- Fat: 30 g.

140. Roasted Trout Stuffed With Veggies

Preparation Time: 10 minutes.
Cooking Time: 25 minutes.
Servings: 2
Ingredient:

- 2 (8 oz.) whole trout fillets.
- 1 tbsp. extra-virgin olive oil.
- ¼ tsp. salt.
- $^1/_8$ tsp. black pepper.
- 1 small onion, thinly sliced.
- ½ red bell pepper.
- 1 poblano pepper.
- 2 or 3 shiitake mushrooms, sliced.
- 1 lemon, sliced.

Directions:

1. Set oven to 425°F (220°C). Coat baking sheet with nonstick cooking spray.
2. Rub both trout fillets inside and out with olive oil. Season with salt and pepper.
3. Mix together the onion, bell pepper, poblano pepper, and mushrooms in a large bowl. Stuff half of this mix into the cavity of each fillet. Top the mixture with 2 or 3 lemon slices inside each fillet.
4. Place the fish on the prepared baking sheet side by side. Roast in the preheated oven for 25 minutes
5. Pull out from the oven and serve on a plate.

Nutrition:

- Calories: 453.
- Fat: 22 g.
- Protein: 49 g.

141. Lemony Trout With Caramelized Shallots

Preparation Time: 10 minutes.
Cooking Time: 20 minutes.
Servings: 2
Ingredients:
For the shallots:

- 1 tsp. almond butter.
- 2 shallots, thinly sliced.
- Dash salt.

For the trout:

- 1 tbsp. almond butter.
- 2 (4 oz./ 113-g.) trout fillets.
- 3 tbsp. capers.
- ¼ cup freshly squeezed lemon juice.
- ¼ tsp. salt.

- Dash freshly ground black pepper.
- 1 lemon, thinly sliced.

Directions:
For shallots:

1. Situate skillet over medium heat, cook the butter, shallots, and salt for 20 minutes, stirring every 5 minutes.

For trout:

1. Meanwhile, in another large skillet over medium heat, heat 1 tsp. of almond butter.
2. Add the trout fillets and cook each side for 3 minutes, or until flaky. Transfer to a plate and set aside.
3. In the skillet used for the trout, stir in the capers, lemon juice, salt, and pepper, then bring to a simmer. Whisk in the remaining 1 tbsp. of almond butter. Spoon the sauce over the fish.
4. Garnish the fish with lemon slices and caramelized shallots before serving.

Nutrition:

- Calories: 344.
- Protein: 21 g.
- Fat: 18 g.

142. Mackerel and Green Bean Salad

Preparation Time: 10 minutes.
Cooking Time: 10 minutes.
Servings: 2
Ingredients:

- 2 cups green beans.
- 1 tbsp. avocado oil.
- 2 mackerel fillets.
- 4 cups mixed salad greens.
- 2 hard-boiled eggs, sliced.
- 1 avocado, sliced.
- 2 tbsp. lemon juice.
- 2 tbsp. olive oil.
- 1 tsp. Dijon mustard.
- Salt and black pepper, to taste.

Directions:

1. Cook the green beans in a pot of boiling water for about 3 minutes. Drain and set aside.
2. Melt the avocado oil in a pan over medium heat. Add the mackerel fillets and cook each side for 4 minutes.
3. Divide the greens between two salad bowls. Top with the mackerel, sliced egg, and avocado slices.

4. Scourge lemon juice, olive oil, mustard, salt, and pepper, and drizzle over the salad. Add the cooked green beans and toss to combine, then serve.

Nutrition:
- Calories: 737.
- Fat: 57 g.
- Protein: 34 g.

143. Hazelnut Crusted Sea Bass

Preparation Time: 10 minutes.
Cooking Time: 15 minutes.
Servings: 2
Ingredients:
- 2 tbsp. almond butter.
- 2 sea bass fillets.
- $1/_3$ cup roasted hazelnuts.
- A pinch cayenne pepper.

Directions:
1. Ready oven to 425°F (220°C). Line a baking dish with waxed paper.
2. Brush the almond butter over the fillets.
3. Pulse the hazelnuts and cayenne in a food processor. Coat the sea bass with the hazelnut mixture, then transfer to the baking dish.
4. Bake in the preheated oven for about 15 minutes. Cool for 5 minutes before serving.

Nutrition:
- Calories: 468.
- Fat: 31 g.
- Protein: 40 g.

144. Salmon Baked in Foil

Preparation Time: 5 minutes.
Cooking Time: 25 minutes.
Servings: 4
Ingredients:
- 2 cups cherry tomatoes.
- 3 tbsp. extra-virgin olive oil.
- 3 tbsp. lemon juice.
- 3 tbsp. almond butter.
- 1 tsp. oregano.
- ½ tsp. salt.
- 4 (5 oz. / 142-g.) salmon fillets.

Directions:
1. Preheat the oven to 400°F (205°C). Cut the tomatoes in half and put them in a bowl. Add the olive oil, lemon juice, butter, oregano, and salt to the tomatoes and gently toss to combine.
2. Cut 4 pieces of foil, about 12-by-12 inches each. Place the salmon fillets in the middle of each piece of foil.
3. Divide the tomato mixture evenly over the 4 pieces of salmon. Bring the ends of the foil together and seal to form a closed pocket.
4. Place the 4 pockets on a baking sheet. Bake in the preheated oven for 25 minutes. Remove from the oven and serve on a plate.

Nutrition:
- Calories: 410.
- Protein: 30.0 g.
- Fat: 32.0 g.
- Carbs: 4.0 g.

145. Instant Pot Poached Salmon

Preparation Time: 10 minutes.
Cooking Time: 3 minutes.
Servings: 4
Ingredients:
- 1 lemon, sliced ¼ inch thick.
- 4 (6 oz./ 170-g.) skinless salmon fillets, 1½ inches thick.
- ½ tsp. salt.
- ¼ tsp. pepper.
- ½ cup water.

Directions:
1. Layer the lemon slices in the bottom of the Instant Pot. Season the salmon with salt and pepper, then arrange the salmon (skin-side down) on top of the lemon slices. Pour in the water.
2. Secure the lid. Select the Manual mode and set the Cooking Time for 3 minutes at High Pressure. Once cooking is complete, do a quick pressure release. Carefully open the lid. Serve warm.

Nutrition:
- Calories: 350. Protein: 35.0 g.
- Fat: 23.0 g.
- Carbs: 0 g.

146. Balsamic-Honey Glazed Salmon

Preparation Time: 5 minutes.
Cooking Time: 8 minutes.
Servings: 4
Ingredients:

- ½ cup balsamic vinegar.
- 1 tbsp. honey.
- 4 (8 oz./ 227-g.) salmon fillets.
- Sea salt and freshly ground pepper, to taste.
- 1 tbsp. olive oil.

Directions:

1. Heat a skillet over medium-high heat. Combine the vinegar and honey in a small bowl. Season the salmon fillets with sea salt and freshly ground pepper; brush with the honey-balsamic glaze.
2. Add olive oil to the skillet, and sear the salmon fillets, cooking for 3 to 4 minutes on each side until lightly browned and medium-rare in the center. Let sit for 5 minutes before serving.

Nutrition:

- Calories: 454.
- Protein: 65.3 g.
- Fat: 17.3 g.
- Carbs: 9.7 g.

147. Seared Salmon With Lemon Cream Sauce

Preparation Time: 10 minutes.
Cooking Time: 20 minutes.
Servings: 4
Ingredients:

- 4 (5 oz./ 142-g.) salmon fillets.
- Sea salt and freshly ground black pepper, to taste.
- 1 tbsp. extra-virgin olive oil.
- ½ cup low-Sodium vegetable broth.
- Juice and zest 1 lemon.
- 1 tsp. chopped fresh thyme.
- ½ cup Fat-free sour cream.
- 1 tsp. honey.
- 1 tbsp. chopped fresh chives.

Directions:

1. Preheat the oven to 400°F (205°C). Season the salmon lightly on both sides with salt and pepper. Place a large ovenproof skillet over medium-high heat and add the olive oil.
2. Sear the salmon fillets on both sides until golden, about 3 minutes per side. Transfer the salmon to a baking dish and bake in the preheated oven until just cooked through about 10 minutes.
3. Meanwhile, whisk together the vegetable broth, lemon juice and zest, and thyme in a small saucepan over medium-high heat until the liquid reduces by about one-quarter, about 5 minutes.
4. Whisk in the sour cream and honey. Stir in the chives and serve the sauce over the salmon.

Nutrition:

- Calories: 310.
- Protein: 29.0 g.
- Fat: 18.0 g.
- Carbs: 6.0 g.

148. Tuna and Zucchini Patties

Preparation Time: 15 minutes.
Cooking Time: 12 minutes.
Servings: 4
Ingredients:

- 3 slices whole-wheat sandwich bread, toasted.
- 2 (5 oz./ 142-g.) cans tuna in olive oil, drained.
- 1 cup shredded zucchini.
- 1 large egg, lightly beaten.
- ¼ cup diced red bell pepper.
- 1 tbsp. dried oregano.
- 1 tsp. lemon zest.
- ¼ tsp. freshly ground black pepper.
- ¼ tsp. kosher or sea salt.
- 1 tbsp. extra-virgin olive oil.
- Salad greens or 4 whole-wheat rolls, for serving (optional).

Directions:

1. Crumble the toast into bread crumbs with your fingers (or use a knife to cut into ¼-inch cubes) until you have 1 cup of loosely packed crumbs.
2. Pour the crumbs into a large bowl. Add the tuna, zucchini, beaten egg, bell pepper,

oregano, lemon zest, black pepper, and salt. Mix well with a fork.

3. With your hands, form the mixture into four (½-cup-size) patties. Place them on a plate and press each patty flat to about ¾-inch thick.

4. In a large skillet over medium-high heat, heat the oil until it's very hot, about 2 minutes. Add the patties to the hot oil, then reduce the heat down to medium.

5. Cook the patties for 5 minutes, flip with a spatula, and cook for an additional 5 minutes. Serve the patties on salad greens or whole-wheat rolls, if desired.

Nutrition:
- Calories: 757.
- Protein: 5.0 g.
- Fat: 72.0 g.
- Carbs: 26.0 g.

149. Fennel Poached Cod With Tomatoes

Preparation Time: 15 minutes.
Cooking Time: 20 minutes.
Servings: 4
Ingredients:
- 1 tbsp. olive oil.
- 1 cup thinly sliced fennel.
- ½ cup thinly sliced onion.
- 1 tbsp. minced garlic.
- 1 (15 oz./ 425-g.) can diced tomatoes.
- 2 cups chicken broth.
- ½ cup white wine.
- Juice and zest 1 orange.
- 1 pinch red pepper flakes.
- 1 bay leaf.
- 1 pound (454 g) cod.

Directions:
1. Heat the olive oil in a large skillet. Add the onion and fennel and cook for 6 minutes, stirring occasionally, or until translucent. Add the garlic and cook for 1 minute more.

2. Add the tomatoes, chicken broth, wine, orange juice and zest, red pepper flakes, and bay leaf, and simmer for 5 minutes to meld the flavors.

3. Carefully add the cod in a single layer, cover, and simmer for 6 to 7 minutes. Transfer fish to a serving dish, ladle the remaining sauce over the fish, and serve.

Nutrition:
- Calories: 336.
- Protein: 45.1 g.
- Fat: 12.5 g.
- Carbs: 11.0 g.

150. Baked Fish With Pistachio Crust

Preparation Time: 15 minutes.
Cooking Time: 15 to 20 minutes.
Servings: 4
Ingredients:
- ½ cup extra-virgin olive oil, divided.
- 1 pound (454 g) flaky white fish (such as cod, haddock, or halibut), skin removed.
- ½ cup shelled finely chopped pistachios.
- ½ cup ground flaxseed.
- Zest and juice 1 lemon, divided.
- 1 tsp. ground cumin.
- 1 tsp. ground allspice.
- ½ tsp. salt.
- ¼ tsp. freshly ground black pepper.

Directions:
1. Preheat the oven to 400°F (205°C). Line a baking sheet with parchment paper or aluminum foil and drizzle 2 tbsp. of olive oil over the sheet, spreading to evenly coat the bottom.

2. Cut the fish into 4 equal pieces and place them on the prepared baking sheet.

3. In a small bowl, combine the pistachios, flaxseed, lemon zest, cumin, allspice, salt, and pepper. Drizzle in ¼ cup of olive oil and stir well.

4. Divide the nut mixture evenly on top of the fish pieces. Drizzle the lemon juice and remaining 2 tbsp. of olive oil over the fish and bake until cooked through, 15 to 20 minutes, depending on the thickness of the fish. Cool for 5 minutes before serving.

Nutrition:
- Calories: 509. Protein: 26.0 g.
- Fat: 41.0 g. Carbs: 9.0 g.

151. Dill Baked Sea Bass

Preparation Time: 15 minutes.
Cooking Time: 10 to 15 minutes.
Servings: 6
Ingredients:
- ¼ cup olive oil.
- 2 pounds (907 g.) sea bass.

- Sea salt and freshly ground pepper, to taste.
- 1 garlic clove, minced.
- ¼ cup dry white wine.
- 3 tsp. fresh dill.
- 2 tsp. fresh thyme.

Directions:

1. Preheat the oven to 425°F (220°C). Brush the bottom of a roasting pan with olive oil. Place the fish in the pan and brush the fish with oil.
2. Season the fish with sea salt and freshly ground pepper. Combine the remaining Ingredients and pour over the fish.
3. Bake in the preheated oven for 10 to 15 minutes, depending on the size of the fish. Serve hot.

Nutrition:

- Calories: 224. Protein: 28.1 g.
- Fat: 12.1 g. Carbs: 0.9 g.

152. Sole Piccata With Capers

Preparation Time: 15 minutes.
Cooking Time: 17 minutes.
Servings: 4
Ingredients:

- 1 tsp. extra-virgin olive oil.
- 4 (5 oz./ 142-g.) sole fillets, patted dry.
- 3 tbsp. almond butter.
- 2 tsp. minced garlic.
- 2 tbsp. all-purpose flour.
- 2 cups low-Sodium chicken broth.
- Juice and zest ½ lemon.
- 2 tbsp. capers.

Directions:

1. Place a large skillet over medium-high heat and add the olive oil. Sear the sole fillets until the fish flakes easily when tested with a fork, about 4 minutes on each side. Transfer the fish to a plate and set it aside.
2. Return the skillet to the stove and add the butter. Sauté the garlic until translucent, about 3 minutes.
3. Whisk in the flour to make a thick paste and cook, stirring constantly, until the mixture is golden brown, about 2 minutes.
4. Whisk in the chicken broth, lemon juice, and zest. Cook for about 4 minutes until the sauce is thickened. Stir in the capers and serve the sauce over the fish.

Nutrition:

- Calories: 271. Protein: 30.0 g.
- Fat: 13.0 g. Carbs: 7.0 g.

153. Haddock With Cucumber Sauce

Preparation Time: 15 minutes.
Cooking Time: 10 minutes.
Servings: 4
Ingredients:

- ¼ cup plain Greek yogurt.
- ½ scallion, white and green parts, finely chopped.
- ½ English cucumber, grated, liquid squeezed out.
- 2 tsp. chopped fresh mint.
- 1 tsp. honey.
- Sea salt and freshly ground black pepper, to taste.
- 4 (5 oz./ 142-g.) haddock fillets, patted dry.
- Nonstick cooking spray.

Directions:

1. In a small bowl, stir together the yogurt, cucumber, scallion, mint, honey, and a pinch of salt. Set aside. Season the fillets lightly with salt and pepper.
2. Place a large skillet over medium-high heat and spray lightly with cooking spray. Cook the haddock, turning once until it is just cooked through, about 5 minutes per side.
3. Remove the fish from the heat and transfer them to plates. Serve topped with the cucumber sauce.

Nutrition:

- Calories: 164. Protein: 27.0 g.
- Fat: 2.0 g. Carbs: 4.0 g.

154. Crispy Herb Crusted Halibut

Preparation Time: 15 minutes.
Cooking Time: 20 minutes.
Servings: 4
Ingredients:

- 4 (5 oz./142-g.) halibut fillets, patted dry.

- Extra-virgin olive oil, for brushing.
- ½ cup coarsely ground unsalted pistachios.
- 1 tbsp. chopped fresh parsley.
- 1 tsp. chopped fresh basil.
- 1 tsp. chopped fresh thyme.
- Pinch sea salt.
- Pinch freshly ground black pepper.

Directions:

1. Preheat the oven to 350°F (180°C). Line a baking sheet with parchment paper. Place the fillets on the baking sheet and brush them generously with olive oil.
2. In a small bowl, stir together the pistachios, parsley, basil, thyme, salt, and pepper. Spoon the nut mixture evenly on the fish, spreading it out so the tops of the fillets are covered.
3. Bake in the preheated oven until it flakes when pressed with a fork, about 20 minutes. Serve immediately.

Nutrition:

- Calories: 262.
- Protein: 32.0 g.
- Fat: 11.0 g.
- Carbs: 4.0 g.

155. Pasta With Cherry Tomatoes and Anchovies

Preparation Time: 15 minutes.
Cooking Time: 20 minutes.
Servings: 5
Ingredients:

- 10 ½ oz. spaghetti.
- 1 ⅛ pound cherry tomatoes.
- 9 oz. anchovies (pre-cleaned).
- 2 tbsp. capers.
- 1 garlic clove.
- 1 small red onion.
- Parsley to taste.
- Extra virgin olive oil to taste.
- Table salt to taste.
- Black pepper to taste.
- Black olives to taste.

Directions:

1. Cut the garlic clove, obtaining thin slices. Cut the cherry tomatoes in 2. Peel the onion and slice it thinly.
2. Put a little oil with the sliced garlic and onions in a saucepan. Heat everything over medium heat for 5 minutes; stir occasionally.

3. Once everything has been well flavored, add the cherry tomatoes and a pinch of salt and pepper. Cook for 15 minutes.
4. Meanwhile, put a pot of water on the stove and as soon as it boils, add the salt and the pasta. Once the sauce is almost ready, add the anchovies and cook for a couple of minutes. Stir gently.
5. Turn off the heat, chop the parsley and place it in the pan. When the pasta is cooked, strain it and add it directly to the sauce. Turn the heat back on again for a few seconds. Serve.

Nutrition:

- Calories: 446.
- Protein: 22.8 g.
- Fat: 10 g.
- Carbs: 66.1 g.

156. Mussels With Tomatoes & Chili

Preparation Time: 15 minutes.
Cooking Time: 12 minutes.
Servings: 4
Ingredients:

- 2 ripe tomatoes.
- 2 tbsp. olive oil.
- 1 tsp. tomato paste.
- 1 garlic clove, chopped.
- 1 shallot, chopped.
- 1 chopped red or green chili.
- Small glass dry white wine.
- Salt and pepper to taste.
- 2 pounds /900 g. mussels, cleaned.
- Basil leaves, fresh.

Directions:

1. Add tomatoes to boiling water for 3 minutes then drain. Peel the tomatoes and chop the flesh. Add oil to an iron skillet and heat to sauté shallots and garlic for 3 minutes.
2. Stir in wine along with tomatoes, chili, salt/pepper, and tomato paste. Cook for 2 minutes then add mussels. Cover and let it steam for 4 minutes. Garnish with basil leaves and serve warm.

Nutrition:

- Calories: 483.
- Protein: 62.3 g.
- Fat: 15.2 g.
- Carbs: 20.4 g.

157. Lemon Garlic Shrimp

Preparation Time: 15 minutes.
Cooking Time: 10 minutes.
Servings: 6
Ingredients:

- 4 tsp. extra-virgin olive oil, divided.
- 2 red bell peppers, diced.
- 2 pounds /900 g. fresh asparagus, sliced.
- 2 tsp. lemon zest, freshly grated.
- ½ tsp. salt, divided.
- 5 garlic cloves, minced.
- 1 pound/450 g. peeled raw shrimp, deveined.
- 1 cup reduced-Sodium chicken broth or water.
- 1 tsp. cornstarch.
- 2 tbsp. lemon juice.
- 2 tbsp. fresh parsley, chopped.

Directions:

1. Add 2 tsp. of oil to a large skillet and heat for a minute. Stir in asparagus, lemon zest, bell pepper, and salt. Sauté for 6 minutes.
2. Keep the sautéed veggies in a separate bowl. Add remaining oil to the same pan and add garlic. Sauté for 30 seconds then add shrimp. Cook for 1 minute.
3. Mix cornstarch with broth in a bowl and pour this mixture into the pan. Add salt and stir cook for 2 minutes. Turn off flame then add parsley and lemon juice. Serve warm with sautéed vegetables.

Nutrition:

- Calories: 204.
- Protein: 17. 1 g.
- Fat: 4 g.
- Carbs: 23.6 g.

158. Pepper Tilapia With Spinach

Preparation Time: 15 minutes.
Cooking Time: 27 minutes.
Servings: 4
Ingredients:

- 4 tilapia fillets, 8 oz./ 227 g. each.
- 4 cups fresh spinach.
- 1 red onion, sliced.
- 3 garlic cloves, minced.
- 2 tbsp. extra virgin olive oil.
- 3 lemons.
- 1 tbsp. ground black pepper.

- 1 tbsp. ground white pepper.
- 1 tbsp. crushed red pepper.

Directions:

1. Set the oven to preheat at 350°F/176.6° C. Place the fish in a shallow baking dish and juice two of the lemons.
2. Cover the fish in the lemon juice and then sprinkle the three types of pepper over the fish. Slice the remaining lemon and cover the fish. Bake in the oven for 20 minutes.
3. While the fish cooks, sauté the garlic and onion in olive oil. Add the spinach and sauté for 7 more minutes. Top the fish with spinach and serve.

Nutrition:

- Calories: 323.
- Protein: 50 g.
- Fat: 11.4 g.
- Carbs: 10.4 g.

159. Spicy Shrimp Salad

Preparation Time: 15 minutes.
Cooking Time: 0 minutes.
Servings: 2
Ingredients:

- ½ pound salad shrimp, chopped.
- 2 stalks celery, chopped.
- ¼ cup red onion, diced.
- 1 tsp. black pepper.
- 1 tsp. red pepper.
- 1 tbsp. lemon juice.
- Dash cayenne pepper.
- 1 tbsp. olive oil.
- 2 cucumbers, sliced.

Directions:

1. Combine the shrimp, celery, and onion in a bowl and mix together. In a separate bowl, whisk the oil and the lemon juice, then add red pepper, black pepper, and cayenne pepper.
2. Pour over the shrimp and mix. Serve with slices of thickly cut cucumber on it and enjoy.

Nutrition:

- Calories: 245.
- Protein: 27.3 g.
- Fat: 9 g.
- Carbs: 18.2 g.

160. Baked Cod in Parchment

Preparation Time: 15 minutes.

Cooking Time: 0 minutes.

Servings: 1

Ingredients:

- 1 to 2 potatoes, sliced.
- 5 cherry tomatoes, halved.
- 5 pitted olives.
- Juice ½ lemon.
- ½ tbsp. olive oil.
- 4 oz. cod.
- 20 inches long parchment.
- Sea salt and black pepper.

Directions:

1. Set your oven to preheat at 350°F/176.6° C. Spread the olive oil on parchment and arrange potato on it.
2. In a separate bowl combine the tomatoes, olives, and lemon juice. Put the fish fillet on potatoes and top with tomato mixture. Add salt and pepper. Fold the filled parchment squares and bake for 20 minutes.

Nutrition:

- Calories: 330.
- Protein: 25 g.
- Fat: 8 g.
- Carbs: 35 g.

CHAPTER 14:

Snacks and Dessert Recipes

161. Berry and Rhubarb Cobbler

Preparation Time: 15 minutes.

Cooking Time: 35 minutes.

Servings: 8

Ingredients:

For the cobbler:

- 1 cup fresh raspberries.
- 2 cups fresh blueberries.
- 1 cup sliced (½-inch) rhubarb pieces.
- 1 tbsp. arrowroot powder.
- ¼ cup unsweetened apple juice.
- 2 tbsp. melted coconut oil.
- ¼ cup raw honey.

For the topping:

- 1 cup almond flour.
- 1 tbsp. arrowroot powder.
- ½ cup shredded coconut.
- ¼ cup raw honey.
- ½ cup coconut oil.

Directions:

1. Preheat the oven to 350°F (180°C). Grease a baking dish with melted coconut oil. Combine the Ingredients for the cobbler in a large bowl. Stir to mix well. Spread the mixture in a single layer on the baking dish. Set aside.
2. Combine the almond flour, arrowroot powder, and coconut in a bowl. Stir to mix well. Fold in the honey and coconut oil. Stir with a fork until the mixture crumbled.
3. Spread the topping over the cobbler, then bake in the preheated oven for 35 minutes or until frothy and golden brown. Serve immediately.

Nutrition:

- Calories: 305.
- Protein: 3.2 g.
- Fat: 22.1g.
- Carbs: 29.8g.

162. Citrus Cranberry and Quinoa Energy Bites

Preparation Time: 15 minutes.

Cooking Time: 0 minutes.

Servings: 12 bites.

Ingredients:

- 2 tbsp. almond butter.
- 2 tbsp. maple syrup.
- ¾ cup cooked quinoa.
- 1 tbsp. dried cranberries.
- 1 tbsp. chia seeds.
- ¼ cup ground almonds.
- ¼ cup sesame seeds, toasted.
- Zest 1 orange.
- ½ tsp. vanilla extract.

Directions:

1. Line a baking sheet with parchment paper. Combine the butter and maple syrup in a bowl. Stir to mix well.
2. Fold in the remaining Ingredients and stir until the mixture holds together and smooth. Divide the mixture into 12 equal parts, then shape each part into a ball.
3. Arrange the balls on the baking sheet, then refrigerate for at least 15 minutes. Serve chilled.

Nutrition:

- Calories: 110.
- Protein: 3.1 g.
- Fat: 10.8g.
- Carbs: 4.9g.

163. Chocolate, Almond, and Cherry Clusters

Preparation Time: 15 minutes.

Cooking Time: 3 minutes.

Servings: 10 clusters.

Ingredients:

- 1 cup dark chocolate (60% cocoa or higher), chopped.
- 1 tbsp. coconut oil.
- ½ cup dried cherries.
- 1 cup roasted salted almonds.

Directions:

1. Line a baking sheet with parchment paper. Melt the chocolate and coconut oil in a saucepan for 3 minutes. Stir constantly.
2. Turn off the heat and mix in the cherries and almonds. Drop the mixture on the baking sheet with a spoon. Place the sheet in the

refrigerator and chill for at least 1 hour or until firm. Serve chilled.

Nutrition:
- Calories: 197.
- Protein: 4.1 g.
- Fat: 13.2g.
- Carbs: 17.8g.

164. Apple and Berries Ambrosia

Preparation Time: 15 minutes.

Cooking Time: 0 minutes.

Servings: 4

Ingredients:
- 2 cups unsweetened coconut milk, chilled.
- 2 tbsp. raw honey
- 1 apple, peeled, cored, and chopped.
- 2 cups fresh raspberries.
- 2 cups fresh blueberries.

Directions:
1. Spoon the chilled milk in a large bowl, then mix in the honey. Stir to mix well.
2. Then mix in the remaining Ingredients. Stir to coat the fruits well and serve immediately.

Nutrition:
- Calories: 386.
- Protein: 4.2 g.
- Fat: 21.1g.
- Carbs: 45.9g.

165. Chocolate and Avocado Mousse

Preparation Time: 15 minutes.

Cooking Time: 5 minutes.

Servings: 4 to 6

Ingredients:
- 8 oz. (227 g) dark chocolate (60% cocoa or higher), chopped.
- ¼ cup unsweetened coconut milk.
- 2 tbsp. coconut oil.
- 2 ripe avocados, deseeded.
- ¼ cup raw honey.
- Sea salt, to taste.

Directions:
1. Put the chocolate in a saucepan. Pour in the coconut milk and add the coconut oil. Cook for 3 minutes or until the chocolate and coconut oil melt. Stir constantly.
2. Put the avocado in a food processor, then drizzle with honey and melted chocolate. Pulse to combine until smooth.
3. Pour the mixture into a serving bowl, then sprinkle with salt. Refrigerate to chill for 30 minutes and serve.

Nutrition:
- Calories: 654.
- Protein: 7.2 g.
- Fat: 46.8g.
- Carbs: 55.9g.

166. Coconut Blueberries With Brown Rice

Preparation Time: 15 minutes.

Cooking Time: 10 minutes.

Servings: 4

Ingredients:
- 1 cup fresh blueberries.
- 2 cups unsweetened coconut milk.
- 1 tsp. ground ginger.
- ¼ cup maple syrup.
- Sea salt, to taste.
- 2 cups cooked brown rice.

Directions:
1. Put all the Ingredients, except for the brown rice, in a pot. Stir to combine well. Cook over medium-high heat for 7 minutes or until the blueberries are tender.
2. Pour in the brown rice and cook for 3 more minutes or until the rice is soft. Stir constantly. Serve immediately.

Nutrition:
- Calories: 470. Protein: 6.2 g.
- Fat: 24.8g. Carbs: 60.1g.

167. Easy Blueberry and Oat Crisp

Preparation Time: 15 minutes.

Cooking Time: 20 minutes.

Servings: 4

Ingredients:
- 2 tbsp. coconut oil, melted, plus additional for greasing.

- 4 cups fresh blueberries.
- Juice ½ lemon.
- 2 tsp. lemon zest.
- ¼ cup maple syrup.
- 1 cup gluten-free rolled oats.
- ½ cup chopped pecans.
- ½ tsp. ground cinnamon.
- Sea salt, to taste.

Directions:

1. Preheat the oven to 350°F (180°C). Grease a baking sheet with coconut oil. Combine the blueberries, lemon juice and zest, and maple syrup in a bowl. Stir to mix well, then spread the mixture on the baking sheet.
2. Combine the remaining Ingredients in a small bowl. Stir to mix well. Pour the mixture over the blueberry mixture.
3. Bake in the preheated oven for 20 minutes or until the oats are golden brown. Serve immediately with spoons.

Nutrition:

- Calories: 496.
- Protein: 5.1 g.
- Fat: 32.9g.
- Carbs: 50.8g.

168. Glazed Pears With Hazelnuts

Preparation Time: 15 minutes.
Cooking Time: 20 minutes.
Servings: 4
Ingredients:

- 4 pears, peeled, cored, and quartered lengthwise.
- 1 cup apple juice.
- 1 tbsp. grated fresh ginger.
- ½ cup pure maple syrup.
- ¼ cup chopped hazelnuts.

Directions:

1. Put the pears in a pot, then pour in the apple juice. Bring to a boil over medium-high heat, then reduce the heat to medium-low. Stir constantly.
2. Cover and simmer for an additional 15 minutes or until the pears are tender.
3. Meanwhile, combine the ginger and maple syrup in a saucepan. Bring to a boil over medium-high heat. Stir frequently. Turn off the heat and transfer the syrup to a small bowl and let sit until ready to use.

4. Transfer the pears to a large serving bowl with a slotted spoon, then top the pears with syrup. Spread the hazelnuts over the pears and serve immediately.

Nutrition:

- Calories: 287.
- Protein: 2.2 g.
- Fat: 3.1g.
- Carbs: 66.9g.

169. Lemony Blackberry Granita

Preparation Time: 15 minutes.
Cooking Time: 0 minutes.
Servings: 4
Ingredients:

- 1 pound (454 g) fresh blackberries.
- 1 tsp. chopped fresh thyme.
- ¼ cup freshly squeezed lemon juice.
- ½ cup raw honey.
- ½ cup water.

Directions:

1. Put all the Ingredients in a food processor, then pulse to purée. Pour the mixture through a sieve into a baking dish. Discard the seeds that remain in the sieve.
2. Put the baking dish in the freezer for 2 hours. Remove the dish from the refrigerator and stir to break any frozen parts.
3. Return the dish back to the freezer for an hour, then stir to break any frozen parts again. Return the dish to the freezer for 4 hours until the granita is completely frozen.
4. Remove it from the freezer and mash to serve.

Nutrition:

- Calories: 183.
- Protein: 2.2 g.
- Fat: 1.1g.
- Carbs: 45.9g.

170. Cucumber Sandwich Bites

Preparation Time: 5 minutes.
Cooking Time: 0 minutes.
Servings: 12
Ingredients:

- 1 cucumber, sliced.
- 8 slices whole-wheat bread.
- 2 tbsp. cream cheese, soft.
- 1 tbsp. chives, chopped.
- ¼ cup avocado, peeled, pitted, and mashed.
- 1 tsp. mustard.
- Salt and black pepper to the taste.

Directions:

1. Spread the mashed avocado on each bread slice, also spread the rest of the Ingredients except the cucumber slices.
2. Divide the cucumber slices into the bread slices, cut each slice in thirds, arrange on a platter and serve as an appetizer.

Nutrition:

- Calories: 187.
- Protein: 8.2 g.
- Fat: 12.4g.
- Carbs: 4.5g.

171. Yogurt Dip

Preparation Time: 10 minutes.
Cooking Time: 0 minutes.
Servings: 6
Ingredients:

- 2 cups Greek yogurt.
- 2 tbsp. pistachios, toasted and chopped.
- A pinch salt and white pepper.
- 2 tbsp. mint, chopped.
- 1 tbsp. kalamata olives, pitted and chopped.
- ¼ cup zaatar spice.
- ¼ cup pomegranate seeds.
- $^1/_3$ cup olive oil.

Directions:

1. Mix the yogurt with the pistachios and the rest of the Ingredients, whisk well, divide into small cups and serve with pita chips on the side.

Nutrition:

- Calories: 294. Protein: 10 g.
- Fat: 18g. Carbs: 2g.

172. Tomato Bruschetta

Preparation Time: 10 minutes.
Cooking Time: 10 minutes.
Servings: 6
Ingredients:

- 1 baguette, sliced.
- $^1/_3$ cup basil, chopped.
- 6 tomatoes, cubed.
- 2 garlic cloves, minced.
- A pinch salt and black pepper.
- 1 tsp. olive oil.
- 1 tbsp. balsamic vinegar.
- ½ tsp. garlic powder.
- Cooking spray.

Directions:

1. Situate the baguette slices on a baking sheet lined with parchment paper, grease with cooking spray. Bake for 10 minutes at 400°F.
2. Combine the tomatoes with the basil and the remaining Ingredients, toss well and leave aside for 10 minutes. Divide the tomato mix on each baguette slice, arrange them all on a platter and serve.

Nutrition:

- Calories: 162. Protein: 4 g.
- Fat: 4g. Carbs: 29g.

173. Olives and Cheese Stuffed Tomatoes

Preparation Time: 10 minutes.
Cooking Time: 0 minutes.
Servings: 24
Ingredients:

- 24 cherry tomatoes, top cut off, and insides scooped out.
- 2 tbsp. olive oil.
- ¼ tsp. red pepper flakes.
- ½ cup feta cheese, crumbled.
- 2 tbsp. black olive paste.
- ¼ cup mint, torn.

Directions:

1. In a bowl, mix the olives paste with the rest of the Ingredients except the cherry tomatoes and whisk well. Stuff the cherry tomatoes with this mix, arrange them all on a platter, and serve as an appetizer.

Nutrition:

- Calories: 136. Protein: 5.1 g.
- Fat: 8.6g. Carbs: 5.6g.

174. Pepper Tapenade

Preparation Time: 10 minutes.
Cooking Time: 0 minutes.
Servings: 4
Ingredients:

- 7 oz. roasted red peppers, chopped.
- ½ cup parmesan, grated.

- ⅓ cup parsley, chopped.
- 14 oz. canned artichokes, drained and chopped.
- 3 tbsp. olive oil.
- ¼ cup capers, drained.
- 1 ½ tbsp. lemon juice.
- 2 garlic cloves, minced.

Directions:

1. In your blender, combine the red peppers with the parmesan and the rest of the Ingredients and pulse well. Divide into cups and serve as a snack.

Nutrition:

- Calories: 200.
- Protein: 4.6 g.
- Fat: 5.6g. Carbs: 12.4g.

175. Coriander Falafel

Preparation Time: 10 minutes.

Cooking Time: 10 minutes.

Servings: 8

Ingredients:

- 1 cup canned garbanzo beans.
- 1 bunch parsley leaves.
- 1 yellow onion, chopped.
- 5 garlic cloves, minced.
- 1 tsp. coriander, ground.
- A pinch salt and black pepper.
- ¼ tsp. cayenne pepper.
- ¼ tsp. baking soda.
- ¼ tsp. cumin powder.
- 1 tsp. lemon juice.
- 3 tbsp. tapioca flour.
- Olive oil for frying.

Directions:

1. In your food processor, combine the beans with the parsley, onion, and the rest of the Ingredients except the oil and the flour and pulse well.
2. Transfer the mix to a bowl, add the flour, stir well, shape 16 balls out of this mix and flatten them a bit.
3. Preheat pan over medium-high heat, add the falafels, cook them for 5 minutes on both sides, put in paper towels, drain excess grease, arrange them on a platter and serve as an appetizer.

Nutrition:

- Calories: 122. Protein: 3.1 g.
- Fat: 6.2g.
- Carbs: 12.3g.

176. Red Pepper Hummus

Preparation Time: 10 minutes.

Cooking Time: 0 minutes.

Servings: 6

Ingredients:

- 6 oz. roasted red peppers, peeled and chopped.
- 16 oz. canned chickpeas drained and rinsed
- ¼ cup Greek yogurt.
- 3 tbsp. tahini paste.
- Juice 1 lemon.
- 3 garlic cloves, minced.
- 1 tbsp. olive oil.
- A pinch salt and black pepper.
- 1 tbsp. parsley, chopped.

Directions:

1. In your food processor, combine the red peppers with the rest of the Ingredients except the oil and the parsley and pulse well. Add the oil, pulse again, divide into cups, sprinkle the parsley on top, and serve as a party spread.

Nutrition:

- Calories: 255.
- Protein: 6.5 g.
- Fat: 11.4g.
- Carbs: 17.4g.

177. White Bean Dip

Preparation Time: 10 minutes.

Cooking Time: 0 minutes.

Servings: 4

Ingredients:

- 15 oz. canned white beans, drained and rinsed.
- 6 oz. canned artichoke hearts drained and quartered.
- 4 garlic cloves, minced.
- 1 tbsp. basil, chopped.
- 2 tbsp. olive oil.
- Juice ½ lemon.

- Zest ½ lemon, grated.
- Salt and black pepper to the taste.

Directions:

1. In your food processor, combine the beans with the artichokes and the rest of the Ingredients except the oil and pulse well. Add the oil gradually, pulse the mix again, divide into cups and serve as a party dip.

Nutrition:

- Calories: 27.
- Protein: 16.5 g.
- Fat: 11.7g.
- Carbs: 18.5g.

178. Eggplant Dip

Preparation Time: 10 minutes.

Cooking Time: 40 minutes.

Servings: 4

Ingredients:

- 1 eggplant, poked with a fork.
- 2 tbsp. tahini paste.
- 2 tbsp. lemon juice.
- 2 garlic cloves, minced.
- 1 tbsp. olive oil.
- Salt and black pepper to the taste.
- 1 tbsp. parsley, chopped.

Directions:

1. Put the eggplant in a roasting pan, bake at 400°F for 40 minutes, cool down, peel and transfer to your food processor.
2. Blend the rest of the Ingredients except the parsley, pulse well, divide into small bowls and serve as an appetizer with the parsley sprinkled on top.

Nutrition:

- Calories: 121.
- Protein: 4.3 g.
- Fat: 4.3g.
- Carbs: 1.4g.

179. Veggie Fritters

Preparation Time: 10 minutes.

Cooking Time: 10 minutes.

Servings: 8

Ingredients:

- 2 garlic cloves, minced.
- 2 yellow onions, chopped.
- 4 scallions, chopped.
- 2 carrots, grated.
- 2 tsp. cumin, ground.
- ½ tsp. turmeric powder.

- Salt and black pepper to the taste.
- ¼ tsp. coriander, ground.
- 2 tbsp. parsley, chopped.
- ¼ tsp. lemon juice.
- ½ cup almond flour.
- 2 beets, peeled and grated.
- 2 eggs, whisked.
- ¼ cup tapioca flour.
- 3 tbsp. olive oil.

Directions:

1. In a bowl, combine the garlic with the onions, scallions, and the rest of the Ingredients except the oil, stir well and shape medium fritters out of this mix.
2. Preheat pan over medium-high heat, place the fritters, cook for 5 minutes on each side, arrange on a platter and serve.

Nutrition:

- Calories: 209.
- Protein: 4.8 g.
- Fat: 11.2g.
- Carbs: 4.4g.

180. Bulgur Lamb Meatballs

Preparation Time: 10 minutes.

Cooking Time: 15 minutes.

Servings: 6

Ingredients:

- 1 ½ cups Greek yogurt.
- ½ tsp. cumin, ground.
- 1 cup cucumber, shredded.
- ½ tsp. garlic, minced.
- A pinch salt and black pepper.
- 1 cup bulgur.
- 2 cups water.
- 1-pound lamb, ground.
- ¼ cup parsley, chopped.
- ¼ cup shallots, chopped.
- ½ tsp. allspice, ground.
- ½ tsp. cinnamon powder.
- 1 tbsp. olive oil.

Directions:

1. Mix the bulgur with the water, cover the bowl, leave aside for 10 minutes, drain and transfer to a bowl.
2. Add the meat, the yogurt, and the rest of the Ingredients except the oil, stir well and shape medium meatballs out of this mix.
3. Preheat pan over medium-high heat, place the meatballs, cook them for 7 minutes on each

side, arrange them all on a platter and serve as an appetizer.

Nutrition:

- Calories: 300.
- Protein: 6.6 g.
- Fat: 9.6g.
- Carbs: 22.6g.

181. Cucumber Bites

Preparation Time: 10 minutes.

Cooking Time: 0 minutes.

Servings: 12

Ingredients:

- 1 English cucumber, sliced into 32 rounds.
- 10 oz. hummus.
- 16 cherry tomatoes, halved.
- 1 tbsp. parsley, chopped.
- 1 oz. feta cheese, crumbled.

Directions:

1. Spread the hummus on each cucumber round, divide the tomato halves on each, sprinkle the cheese and parsley on to and serve as an appetizer.

Nutrition:

- Calories: 162.
- Protein: 2.4 g.
- Fat: 3.4g.
- Carbs: 6.4g.

182. Stuffed Avocado

Preparation Time: 10 minutes.

Cooking Time: 0 minutes.

Servings: 2

Ingredients:

- 1 avocado, halved and pitted.
- 10 oz. canned tuna, drained.
- 2 tbsp. sun-dried tomatoes, chopped.
- 1 ½ tbsp. basil pesto.
- 2 tbsp. black olives, pitted and chopped.

- Salt and black pepper to the taste.
- 2 tsp. pine nuts, toasted and chopped.
- 1 tbsp. basil, chopped.

Directions:

1. Mix the tuna with the sun-dried tomatoes and the rest of the Ingredients except the avocado and stir. Stuff the avocado halves with the tuna mix and serve as an appetizer.

Nutrition:

- Calories: 233.
- Protein: 5.6 g.
- Fat: 9g.
- Carbs: 11.4g.

183. Wrapped Plums

Preparation Time: 5 minutes.

Cooking Time: 0 minutes.

Servings: 8

Ingredients:

- 2 oz. prosciutto, cut into 16 pieces.
- 4 plums, quartered.
- 1 tbsp. chives, chopped.
- A pinch red pepper flakes, crushed.

Directions:

1. Wrap each plum quarter in a prosciutto slice, arrange them all on a platter, sprinkle the chives and pepper flakes all over, and serve.

Nutrition:

- Calories: 30.
- Protein: 2 g.
- Fat: 1g.
- Carbs: 4g.

184. Marinated Feta and Artichokes

Preparation Time: 10 minutes, plus 4 hours inactive time.

Cooking Time: 10 minutes.

Servings: 2

Ingredients:

- 4 oz. traditional Greek feta, cut into ½-inch cubes.
- 4 oz. drained artichoke hearts quartered lengthwise.
- $^1/_3$ cup extra-virgin olive oil.
- Zest and juice 1 lemon.
- 2 tbsp. roughly chopped fresh rosemary.
- 2 tbsp. roughly chopped fresh parsley.
- ½ tsp. black peppercorns.

Directions:

1. In a glass bowl combine the feta and artichoke hearts. Add the olive oil, lemon zest and juice, rosemary, parsley, and peppercorns, and toss gently to coat, being sure not to crumble the feta.
2. Cool for 4 hours, or up to 4 days. Take out of the refrigerator 30 minutes before serving.

Nutrition:

- Calories: 235.
- Protein: 4 g.
- Fat:23g.
- Carbs: 1g.

185. Tuna Croquettes

Preparation Time: 40 minutes.

Cooking Time: 25 minutes.

Servings: 36

Ingredients:

- 6 tbsp. extra-virgin olive oil, plus 1 to 2 cups.
- 5 tbsp. almond flour, plus 1 cup, divided.
- 1¼ cups heavy cream.
- 1 (4-oz.) can olive oil-packed yellowfin tuna.
- 1 tbsp. chopped red onion.
- 2 tsp. minced capers.
- ½ tsp. dried dill.
- ¼ tsp. freshly ground black pepper.
- 2 large eggs.
- 1 cup panko breadcrumbs (or a gluten-free version).

Directions:

1. In a large skillet, warm up6 tbsp. of olive oil over medium-low heat. Add 5 tbsp. of almond flour and cook, stirring constantly, until a smooth paste forms and the flour browns slightly, 2 to 3 minutes.
2. Select the heat to medium-high and gradually mix in the heavy cream, whisking constantly until completely smooth and thickened,

another 4 to 5 minutes. Remove and add in the tuna, red onion, capers, dill, and pepper.

3. Transfer the mixture to an 8-inch square baking dish that is well coated with olive oil and set aside at room temperature.
4. Wrap and cool for 4 hours or up to overnight. To form the croquettes, set out three bowls. In one, beat together the eggs.
5. In another, add the remaining almond flour. In the third, add the panko. Line a baking sheet with parchment paper.
6. Scoop about a tbsp. of cold prepared dough into the flour mixture and roll to coat. Shake off excess and, using your hands, roll into an oval.
7. Dip the croquette into the beaten egg, then lightly coat in panko. Set on the lined baking sheet and repeat with the remaining dough.
8. In a small saucepan, warm up the remaining 1 to 2 cups of olive oil, over medium-high heat.
9. Once the oil is heated, fry the croquettes 3 or 4 at a time, depending on the size of your pan, removing with a slotted spoon when golden brown.
10. You will need to adjust the temperature of the oil occasionally to prevent burning. If the croquettes get dark brown very quickly, lower the temperature.

Nutrition:

- Calories: 245.
- Protein: 6 g.
- Fat: 22g.
- Carbs: 1g.

186. Smoked Salmon Crudités

Preparation Time: 10 minutes.

Cooking Time: 15 minutes.

Servings: 4

Ingredients:

- 6 oz. smoked wild salmon.
- 2 tbsp. Roasted Garlic Aioli.
- 1 tbsp. Dijon mustard.
- 1 tbsp. chopped scallions, green parts only.
- 2 tsp. chopped capers.
- ½ tsp. dried dill.
- 4 endive spears or hearts of romaine.
- ½ English cucumber, cut into ¼-inch-thick rounds.

Directions:

1. Roughly cut the smoked salmon and transfer in a small bowl. Add the aioli, Dijon, scallions, capers, and dill and mix well.
2. Top endive spears and cucumber rounds with a spoonful of smoked salmon mixture and enjoy chilled.

Nutrition:

- Calories: 92.
- Protein: 9 g.
- Fat: 5g.
- Carbs: 1g.

187. Olive Tapenade With Anchovies

Preparation Time: 1hour and 10 minutes.
Cooking Time: 0 minutes.
Servings: 2
Ingredients:

- 2 cups pitted Klamath olives or other black olives.
- 2 anchovy fillets, chopped.
- 2 tsp. chopped capers.
- 1 garlic clove, finely minced.
- 1 cooked egg yolk.
- 1 tsp. Dijon mustard.
- ¼ cup extra-virgin olive oil.
- Seedy Crackers, Versatile Sandwich Round, or vegetables, for serving (optional).

Directions:

1. Rinse the olives in cold water and drain well. In a food processor, blender, or a large jar (if using an immersion blender) place the drained olives, anchovies, capers, garlic, egg yolk, and Dijon.
2. Process until it forms a thick paste. While running, gradually stream in the olive oil. Handover to a small bowl, cover, and refrigerate for at least 1 hour to let the flavors develop.
3. Serve with Seedy Crackers, atop a Versatile Sandwich Round, or with your favorite crunchy vegetables.

Nutrition:

- Calories: 179.
- Protein: 2 g.
- Fat: 19g.
- Carbs: 2g.

188. Athenian Avgolemono Sour Soup

Preparation Time: 20 minutes.
Cooking Time: 50 minutes.
Servings: 2
Ingredients:

- 8cups water.
- 1pc whole chicken, cut in pieces.
- Salt and pepper.
- 1cup whole grain rice.
- 4pcs eggs, separated.
- 2pcs lemons, juice.
- ¼cup fresh dill, minced.
- Dill sprigs and lemon slices for garnish.

Directions:

1. Pour the water into a large pot. Add the chicken pieces, and cover the pot. Simmer for an hour
2. Remove the cooked chicken pieces from the pot and take 2cups of the chicken broth. Set aside and let it cool
3. Bring to a boil the remaining. Add salt and pepper to taste. Add the rice and cover the pot. Simmer for 20 minutes
4. Meanwhile, de-bone the cooked chicken and tear the flesh into small pieces. Set aside.
5. Work on the separated egg whites and yolks: whisk the egg whites until stiff; whisk the yolks with the lemon juice.
6. Pour the egg yolk mixture into the egg white mixture. Whisk well until fully combined.
7. Add gradually the reserved 2cups of chicken broth to the mixture, whisking constantly to prevent the eggs from curdling.
8. After fully incorporating the egg mixture and chicken broth, pour this mixture into the simmering broth and rice. Add the dill, and stir well. Simmer further without bringing it to a boil.
9. Add the chicken pieces to the soup. Mix until fully combined.
10. To serve, ladle the soup in bowls and sprinkle with fresh ground pepper. Garnish with lemon slices and dill sprigs.

Nutrition:

- Calories: 122.4.
- Protein: 13.7 g.
- Fats: 1.2g.
- Dietary Fiber: 0.2g.
- Carbs: 7.5g.

189. Spring Soup With Gourmet Grains

Preparation Time: 10 minutes.
Cooking Time: 25 minutes.
Servings: 2
Ingredients:

- 2tbsp. olive oil.
- 1pc small onion, diced.
- 6cups chicken broth, homemade (refer to the recipe of Avgolemono Soup).
- 1bay leaf.
- ½cup fresh dill, chopped (divided).
- ⅓cup Italian or Arborio whole grain rice.
- 1cup asparagus, chopped.
- 1cup carrots, diced.
- 1½cups cooked chicken, de-boned and diced or shredded. - ½lemon, juice.
- 1pc large egg.
- 2tbsp. water.
- Kosher salt and fresh pepper to taste.
- Fresh chives, minced for garnish.

Directions:

1. Heat the olive oil and sauté the onions for 5 minutes in a large stockpot placed over medium heat. Pour in the chicken broth.
2. Add the bay leaf and half of the dill. Bring to a boil.
3. Add rice and turn the heat to medium-low. Simmer for 10 minutes.
4. Add the asparagus and carrots. Cook for 15 minutes until the vegetables are tender and the rice cooks through.
5. Add the cooked shredded chicken. Continue simmer over low heat.
6. In the meantime, combine the lemon juice and egg with water in a mixing bowl.
7. Take ½cup of the simmering stock and pour it on the lemon-egg mixture, whisking gradually to prevent eggs from curdling.
8. Pour the lemon-egg broth into the stockpot, still whisking gradually. Soon as the soup thickens, turn off the heat
9. Remove the bay leaf, and discard. Add the remaining dill, salt, and pepper.
10. To serve, ladle the creamy soup into bowls and garnish with minced chives.

Nutrition:

- Calories: 252.8. Protein: 25.6 g.
- Fats: 8g. Dietary Fiber: 0.3g.
- Carbs: 19.8g.

190. Spiced Soup With Lentils & Legumes

Preparation Time: 15 minutes.
Cooking Time: 35 minutes.
Servings: 2
Ingredients:

- 2tbsp. extra-virgin olive oil.
- 2garlic cloves, minced.
- 4pcs large celery stalks, diced.
- 2pcs large onions, diced.
- 6cups water.
- 1tsp. cumin.
- ¾tsp. turmeric.
- ½tsp. cinnamon.
- ½tsp. fresh ginger, grated.
- 1cup dried lentils, rinsed and sorted.
- 116-oz. can chickpeas (garbanzo beans), drained and rinsed.
- 3pcs ripe tomatoes, cubed.
- ½lemon, juice.
- ½ cup fresh cilantro or parsley, chopped.
- Salt.

Directions:

1. Heat the olive oil and sauté the garlic, celery, and onion for 5 minutes in a large stockpot placed over medium heat.
2. Pour in the water. Add the spices and lentils. Cover the stockpot and simmer for 40 minutes until the lentils are tender.
3. Add the chickpeas and tomatoes. (Pour more water and additional spices, if desired.) Simmer for 15 minutes over low heat.
4. Pour in the lemon juice and stir the soup. Add the cilantro or parsley and salt to taste.

Nutrition:

- Calories: 123.
- Protein: 5 g.
- Fats: 3g.
- Dietary Fiber: 5g.
- Carbs: 19g.

191. Dalmatian Cabbage, Potato, And Pea Soup

Preparation Time: 15 minutes.
Cooking Time: 15 minutes.
Servings: 2
Ingredients:

- 4 tbsp. further virgin olive oil.
- 1 Medium onion, chopped.
- 2 tbsp of Carrots, coarsely grated.

- 2 Medium potatoes, peeled and diced into little items inexperienced cabbage, shredded.
- 1 Cup contemporary shelled peas or frozen petit pois.
- ½ Quart water.
- A pinch Salt.
- ½ tbsp Freshly ground black pepper.

Directions

1. Heat the vegetable oil in an exceedingly massive pot and cook the onion over moderate heat for 3 minutes.
2. Add the carrots, potatoes, and cabbage and still cook for an additional 5 minutes.
3. Add the peas and water and produce to a boil.
4. Cowl and simmer for 35 to 40 minutes or till the vegetables are tender and also the soup is fairly thick.
5. Finally, you must season it with salt & black pepper and serve it hot.

Nutrition:

- Calories: 123.
- Protein: 5 g.
- Fats: 3g.
- Dietary Fiber: 5g.
- Carbs: 19g.

192. Mini Nuts and Fruits Crumble

Preparation Time:15 minutes.

Cooking Time:15 minutes.

Servings: 6

Ingredients:

For the topping:

- ¼ cup coarsely chopped hazelnuts.
- 1 cup coarsely chopped walnuts.
- 1 tsp. ground cinnamon.
- Sea salt, to taste.
- 1 tbsp. melted coconut oil.

For the filling:

- 6 fresh figs, quartered.
- 2 nectarines, pitted and sliced.
- 1 cup fresh blueberries.
- 2 tsp. lemon zest.
- ½ cup raw honey.
- 1 tsp. vanilla extract.

Directions:

1. Combine the Ingredients for the topping in a bowl. Stir to mix well. Set aside until ready to use.
2. Preheat the oven to 375°F (190°C). Combine the Ingredients for the fillings in a bowl. Stir to

mix well. Divide the filling into six ramekins, then divide and top with nut topping.

3. Bake in the preheated oven for 15 minutes or until the topping is lightly browned and the filling is frothy. Serve immediately.

Nutrition:

- Calories: 336. Protein: 6.3 g.
- Fat: 18.8g. Carbs: 41.9g.

193. Mint Banana Chocolate Sorbet

Preparation Time: 4 hours & 5 minutes.

Cooking Time: 0 minutes.

Servings: 1

Ingredients:

- 1 frozen banana.
- 1 tbsp. almond butter.
- 2 tbsp. minced fresh mint.
- 2 to 3 tbsp. dark chocolate chips (60% cocoa or higher).
- 2 to 3 tbsp. goji (optional).

Directions:

1. Put the banana, butter, and mint in a food processor. Pulse to purée until creamy and smooth. Add the chocolate and goji, then pulse several more times to combine well.
2. Pour the mixture in a bowl or a ramekin, then freeze for at least 4 hours before serving chilled.

Nutrition:

- Calories: 213. Protein: 3.1 g.
- Fat: 9.8g. Carbs: 2.9g.

194. Pecan and Carrot Cake

Preparation Time: 15 minutes.

Cooking Time: 45 minutes.

Servings: 12

Ingredients:

- ½ cup coconut oil, at room temperature, plus more for greasing the baking dish.
- 2 tsp. pure vanilla extract.

- ¼ cup pure maple syrup.
- 6 eggs.
- ½ cup coconut flour.
- 1 tsp. baking powder.
- 1 tsp. baking soda.
- ½ tsp. ground nutmeg.
- 1 tsp. ground cinnamon.
- $\frac{1}{8}$ tsp. sea salt
- ½ cup chopped pecans.
- 3 cups finely grated carrots.

Directions:

1. Preheat the oven to 350°F (180°C). Grease a 13-by-9-inch baking dish with coconut oil. Combine the vanilla extract, maple syrup, and ½ cup of coconut oil in a large bowl. Stir to mix well.
2. Break the eggs in the bowl and whisk to combine well. Set aside. Combine the coconut flour, baking powder, baking soda, nutmeg, cinnamon, and salt in a separate bowl. Stir to mix well.
3. Make a well in the center of the flour mixture, then pour the egg mixture into the well. Stir to combine well.
4. Add the pecans and carrots to the bowl and toss to mix well. Pour the mixture intoa single layer on the baking dish.
5. Bake in the preheated oven for 45 minutes or until puffed and the cake spring back when lightly press with your fingers.
6. Remove the cake from the oven. Allow to cool for at least 15 minutes, then serve.

Nutrition:

- Calories: 255.
- Protein: 5.1 g.
- Fat: 21.2g.
- Carbs: 12.8g

195. Raspberry Yogurt Basted Cantaloupe

Preparation Time: 15 minutes.
Cooking Time: 0 minutes.
Servings: 6
Ingredients:

- 2 cups fresh raspberries, mashed.
- 1 cup plain coconut yogurt.
- ½ tsp. vanilla extract.
- 1 cantaloupe, peeled and sliced.
- ½ cup toasted coconut flakes.

Directions:

1. Combine the mashed raspberries with yogurt and vanilla extract in a small bowl. Stir to mix well.
2. Place the cantaloupe slices on a platter, then top with the raspberry mixture and spread with toasted coconut. Serve immediately.

Nutrition:

- Calories: 75.
- Protein: 1.2 g.
- Fat: 4.1g.
- Carbs: 10.9g.

196. Simple Apple Compote

Preparation Time: 15 minutes.
Cooking Time: 10 minutes.
Servings: 4
Ingredients:

- 6 apples, peeled, cored, and chopped.
- ¼ cup raw honey.
- 1 tsp. ground cinnamon.
- ¼ cup apple juice.
- Sea salt, to taste.

Directions:

1. Put all the Ingredients in a stockpot. Stir to mix well, then cook over medium-high heat for 10 minutes or until the apples are glazed by honey and lightly saucy. Stir constantly. Serve immediately.

Nutrition:

- Calories: 246. Protein: 1.2 g.
- Fat: 0.9g. Carbs: 66.3g.

197. Peanut Butter and Chocolate Balls

Preparation Time: 45 minutes.
Cooking Time: 0 minutes.
Servings: 15 balls
Ingredients:

- ¾ cup creamy peanut butter.

- ¼ cup unsweetened cocoa powder.
- 2 tbsp. softened almond butter.
- ½ tsp. vanilla extract.
- 1¾ cups maple Sugar.

Directions:

1. Line a baking sheet with parchment paper. Combine all the Ingredients in a bowl. Stir to mix well.
2. Divide the mixture into 15 parts and shape each part into a 1-inch ball. Arrange the balls on the baking sheet and refrigerate for at least 30 minutes, then serve chilled.

Nutrition:

- Calories: 146.
- Protein: 4.2 g.
- Fat: 8.1g.
- Carbs: 16.9g.

198. Spiced Sweet Pecans

Preparation Time: 15 minutes.
Cooking Time: 17 minutes.
Servings: 4
Ingredients:

- 1 cup pecan halves.
- 3 tbsp. almond butter.
- 1 tsp. ground cinnamon.
- ½ tsp. ground nutmeg.
- ¼ cup raw honey.
- ¼ tsp. sea salt.

Directions:

1. Preheat the oven to 350°F (180°C). Line a baking sheet with parchment paper. Combine all the Ingredients in a bowl. Stir to mix well, then spread the mixture in the single layer on the baking sheet with a spatula.
2. Bake in the preheated oven for 16 minutes or until the pecan halves are well browned. Serve immediately.

Nutrition:

- Calories: 324.
- Protein: 3.2 g.
- Fat: 29.8g.
- Carbs: 13.9g.

199. Lemon Crockpot Cake

Preparation Time: 15 minutes.
Cooking Time: 3 hours.
Servings: 8
Ingredients:

- ½ cup coconut flour.
- 1 ½ cup almond flour.
- 3 tbsp. stevia sweetener.
- 2 tsp. baking powder.
- ½ tsp. xanthan gum.
- ½ cup whipping cream.
- ½ cup butter, melted.
- 1 tbsp. juice, freshly squeezed.
- Zest from one large lemon.
- 2 eggs.

Directions:

1. Grease the inside of the crockpot with butter or cooking spray. Mix together coconut flour, almond flour, stevia, baking powder, and xanthan gum in a bowl.
2. In another bowl, combine the whipping cream, butter, lemon juice, lemon zest, and eggs. Mix until well combined.
3. Pour the wet Ingredients into the dry Ingredients gradually and fold to create a smooth batter. Spread the batter in the crockpot and cook on low for 3 hours.

Nutrition:

- Calories: 350.
- Protein: 17.6 g
- Fat: 32.6 g.
- Carbs: 11.1g.

200. Lemon and Watermelon Granita

Preparation Time: 10 minutes + 3 hours to freeze.
Cooking Time: 0 minutes
Servings: 4
Ingredients:

- 4 cups watermelon cubes.
- ¼ cup honey.
- ¼ cup freshly squeezed lemon juice.

Directions:

1. In a blender, combine the watermelon, honey, and lemon juice. Purée all the Ingredients, then pour into a 9-by-9-by-2-inch baking pan and place in the freezer.
2. Every 30 to 60 minutes, run a fork across the frozen surface to fluff and create ice flakes. Freeze for about 3 hours Total and serve.

Nutrition:

- Calories: 153.
- Protein: 2g.
- Fat: 1 g.
- Carbs: 39 g.

Conclusion

Thank you for reading!

Now that you are familiar with the Keto diet on many levels, you should feel confident in your ability to start your own Keto journey. This diet plan isn't going to hinder you or limit you, so do your best to keep this in mind as you begin changing your lifestyle and adjusting your eating habits. Packed with plenty of proteins and good fats, your body is going to go through a transformation as it works to see these things as energy. Before you know it, your body will have an automatically accessible reserve that you can utilize. Whether you need a boost of energy first thing in the morning or a second wind to keep you going throughout the day, this will already be inside of you.

As women grow older, there are a variety of changes occurring within their bodies. Having a great deal of impact, the reduction of estrogen often causes weight gain and a slower metabolism. The keto diet, with adjustments for the particular requirements of women over fifty years old, is a beautiful way to lose weight while relieving some of the aches and pains experienced as the lack of estrogen takes hold. By adapting the diet to make it more palatable for women over the age of 50, the ketogenic diet can be beneficial in more ways than just weight loss. Follow the principles of food choices suggested by studies performed around the world and reap the benefits of this popular diet. Ease into ketosis with the plan outlined, and you will find a smoother transition to a low-carbohydrate lifestyle. Use the tips and tricks to smooth over rough spots and use the food list to try new foods.

While on the Keto diet, you are building up energy stores for your body to utilize. This means that you should be feeling a necessary boost in your energy levels and the ability to get through each moment of each day without struggling. You can say goodbye to the sluggish feeling that often accompanies other diet plans. When you are on Keto, you should only be experiencing the benefits of additional energy and unlimited potential. Your diet isn't going to always feel like a diet. After some time, you will realize that you enjoy eating a Keto menu very much. Because your body will be switching the way it metabolizes, it will also be switching what it craves. Don't be surprised if you end up craving fats and proteins as you progress on the Keto diet—this is what your body will eventually want.

Keto diet helps control blood sugar and improve Nutrition, which in turn not only improves insulin response and resistance but also protects against memory loss, which is often a part of aging.

You have the tools to reach success by losing weight on the keto diet. In the end, the weight loss will be a very generous reward you will enjoy. Thank you once again!